W9-AMC-427

Wyoming's Snake River

Wyoming's Snake River

A River Guide's Chronicle
of People and Places
Plants and Animals

Including a Mile-by-Mile River Log

from Yellowstone National Park

to the Palisades Reservoir

Verne Huser

THE UNIVERSITY OF UTAH PRESS

Salt Lake City

The account of Lt. Gustavus C. Doane first appeared in *Old West* (summer 1994), as "Doane's Snake River Expedition."

Cartography by Heidi H. Hackler
Linocuts by Paul M. Huser

Printed on acid-free paper

06 05 04 03 02 01 00
5 4 3 2 1

LIBRARY OF CONGRESS CATALOGING-IN-PUBLICATION DATA

Huser, Verne.
    Wyoming's Snake River : a river guide's chronicle of people and places, plants and animals : including a mile-by-mile river log from Yellowstone national Park to the Palisades Reservoir / Verne Huser.
        p. cm.
Includes bibliographical references (p.   ) and index.
        ISBN 0-87480-671-2 (pbk. : alk. paper)
    1. Snake River Valley (Wyo.-Wash.)—Description and travel.
2. Snake River Valley (Wyo.-Wash.)—History. 3. Snake River (Wyo.-Wash.)—Description and travel. 5. Natural history—Snake River Valley (Wyo.-Wash.) I. Title.
    F752.S7 H87 2000
    917.96'1—dc21

                                                        00-009383

This book is dedicated to all those who have floated
the Snake River and discovered the high mountain valley
known as Jackson Hole.

May both remain in your memory forever,
inspiring you to appreciate and protect all wild places.

Contents

Acknowledgments

My wholehearted thanks to dozens of Snake River guides and Jackson Hole residents and to family and friends who have helped make this book possible: Dick Allen; Dick Barker; Denny Becker; Tom Bills; Franz Camenzind; Urszula Ciara; Cort Conley; Charlie, Frank, and Shirley Craighead; Bob Dornan; Gene Downer; Brent Eastman; Jim Elder; Betty Erickson; Frank Ewing; Patty Ewing; Jim Griffin; Bill and Tom Guheen; Heidi Hackler; Dave Hansen; Joel Harris; Virginia Heidekoper; Paul Huser; Wayne Johnson; Al Klagge; Inger Koedt; Bonnie Kreps; Ted and Joan Major; Linette Martinez; Pat McCoy; Mardy Murie; George Northup; Breck O'Neil; Tim Palmer; Charlie Sands; Nancy Shea; John Simms; Robert Smith; Byron Tomingas; Harold Turner; and Terry Tempest Williams.

Introduction

If we could soar like an eagle above the windswept ridges of the Continental Divide in northwestern Wyoming, we would see three major river systems: the Yellowstone, which flows into the Missouri–Mississippi River drainage; the Snake, which flows into the Columbia; and the Green, the principal tributary of the Colorado River, which begins in the Wind River Range a few miles to the southeast. This entire mountain complex, encompassing several million acres and protected by two national parks and five national forests, much of it overlaid with designated wilderness, constitutes one of the greatest wildlife sanctuaries south of Canada. This is headwater country.

Rising in high country that comprises southern Yellowstone National Park and the Bridger-Teton Wilderness, the Snake River flows more than a thousand miles before it reaches the Columbia. Two streams begin on the Two Ocean Plateau in southeastern Yellowstone National Park: Atlantic Creek feeds the Yellowstone and Missouri Rivers, ultimately flowing into the Gulf of Mexico, and Pacific Creek feeds the Snake and the Columbia, flowing westward to the Pacific. The Snake River begins in a spring just south of the drainage divide between the two. The Upper Snake flows into Yellowstone through high meadows populated by elk and grizzly bears, and through dense forests where wolverine and fisher dwell, through open willow-bordered parks where beaver dams turn cold meandering streams into trout ponds. It cuts through rugged gorges that hold snow until late summer, past thermal areas that defy winter's cold—areas as wild as any in the forty-eight contiguous states.

These fast-flowing waters, almost as pure as in the days of Jedediah Smith and Jim Bridger (who no doubt sampled them), offer habitat to several species of fish and the insects they feed upon, as well as shorebirds and waterfowl, such as harlequin ducks. Here one finds ouzels or dippers, called "water canaries" by the mountain men who, while working their beaver sets, often heard the dark birds' midwinter song and saw them feed in the pellucid flow. Beaver are abundant, creating wetlands that nourish plants, offering cover and food for an astounding variety of wild creatures.

In its quieter stretches, the river mirrors forests, sunsets, and surrounding peaks on its surface. But this is just one of its guises, for the Snake is a dynamic element of this landscape. It pools in natural lakes and waters the land. It erodes the landscape, carrying sand, silt, and organic debris toward the distant Pacific; it polishes stones and carves its course through solid rock. It undercuts trees and destroys beaver dams during the annual snowmelt runoff, and builds new meadows as the spring floods inundate the land. From one season to the next the river may change its course entirely as it chokes on its own debris, cutting new channels and abandoning old ones, and shortcutting oxbows and depositing new gravel bars, sandbars, and silt beds for next year's crop of young cottonwoods.

Nowhere in the natural landscape can geologic processes be observed more clearly than in a free-flowing river. Landslides and avalanches are more sudden and spectacular. But on a river the whole process of erosion and deposition occurs continually and conspicuously over geologic time, as the river seeks a dynamic equilibrium in its relentless course to the sea. The Upper Snake most dramatically exemplifies all of these natural processes.

Powerful geologic forces have created the landscape we see in the valley below the Teton Range and still operate today, some slowly, others quite suddenly, but all inexorably despite humankind: the work of the Army Corps of Engineers will inevitably be overpowered. Dams, dikes, diversions, and dewatering practices impact the river, but natural forces will ultimately have their way, a fact that becomes evident during every flood year—as it did so profoundly the spring of 1997 when a major side-canyon slide closed U.S. Highway 287 in the Snake River Canyon for several weeks and altered the flow of the Snake River itself. Commercial float trips on the Snake ceased operations for several days during the summers of 1996 and 1997, even in Grand Teton National Park, due to high water.

This book is a guide to understanding the Snake River—any river—as a living, ever changing force and an integral part of the landscape, carving channels, depositing terraces, creating sinuous meanders. The Snake River gives life to the landscape, provides habitat for its wildlife, and offers inspiring vistas to be experienced and remembered.

My own experience with this special place began the summer of 1957 (I was twenty-six at the time). As the recreation director for employees at Jackson Lake Lodge, I worked afternoons and evenings, and had my mornings free and one day off a week to hike wilderness trails, climb the Teton peaks, explore ice caves, discover the Snake River, and develop an interest in natural history. I came alive that summer, and the Snake River was a primary reason.

By late September I had become a boatman; two summers later I had become a professional river guide on the Snake for the Grand Teton Lodge Company. Frank Ewing, who would become one of the major river outfitters on the Snake, was a roommate back then, and Roderick Nash, who became a good friend, went on to write classic books of intellectual and environmental history. We have been running rivers together for decades since.

As young men Frank and I explored the whole wide riverine environment, its fauna and flora, its history and geology. We attended ranger lectures and invited naturalists, park historians, and regional geologists on our float trips. We were trying to gather information to give our float-trip customers a better sense of the Jackson Hole area and the river that helped create it. We never knew who would turn up in our boats: then-secretary of interior Stewart Udall took his first Snake River trip with me in 1961.

I guided on the Snake through 1961, the year I married, and eventually was manager of the Lodge Company's float trip operation. A Fulbright teacher-exchange to Greece took me away from the river for a year, then family matters and teaching kept me away. I became a seasonal ranger naturalist with the National Park Service in Rocky Mountain National Park in Colorado.

Meanwhile, Frank Ewing had gone into the outfitting business, as had longtime Snake River fishing guide Dick Barker. They developed a reciprocal relationship, sending clients to one another when either had a full-capacity day. By 1967 they found they were turning away enough business to fill a third boat, formed a limited partnership, and hired me. I was back on the Snake River, and Barker-Ewing Float Trips had begun.

The decades passed. With eight hundred trips to my credit, I wrote *Snake River Guide*, published in 1972, a modest book so map dependent that when the river changed course, as it does annually, the book eventually became obsolete.

I guided on the Snake until 1973, then moved on to other pursuits. In 1992 I returned to the river, though, guiding another five hundred trips in the mid-1990s. The Snake had changed and so had I, but the experience of floating the river remains much the same, ever changing, ever restorative and illuminating.

Yet change is the constant here as it is everywhere. It is my hope that this book may help you notice these changes and observe in them the continuing natural patterns. In addition to helping you understand the natural forces at work on and near the Snake, I hope this guide enhances your appreciation of the river's flora and fauna and your knowledge of its human history. This is a magical place, but fragile as well. I hope this book increases your awareness of your impact upon it—however lightly you tread, however often you return, however long you stay.

Unless otherwise specified, the terms *left* and *right* appearing in descriptions of features on the shores of the Snake River pertain to the orientation of passengers in watercraft, facing downstream.

Part One

Discovering the River

A History of the Upper Snake River Valley

Prehistory of the Snake

The discovery of the Snake River of course predates the arrival of European and, later, American peoples. According to recent archaeological and anthropological studies, the valley of the Snake River was visited by prehistoric Indians as early as eleven thousand years ago. Just as in historic times, these Paleo-Indians did not reside permanently along the Upper Snake River but did come in seasonally to hunt, fish, and gather medicinal materials and plant foods: seeds, berries, roots, bulbs, and leaves.

Roasting pits for processing roots and bulbs have been found along the northern shores of Jackson Lake, along with such tools as stone grinders, obsidian knives, projectile points, and scrapers. Most who study these early hunter-gatherer people believe they lived on a wide variety of plant foods augmented by meat from deer, elk, bighorn sheep, and occasional bison.

Evidence of "buffalo drops," where small herds were driven over cliffs, exists in the general region. The atlatl, that is, spear-thrower, was a common tool for launching projectiles at large mammals, and juniper-bark nets were used to capture bighorn sheep. Grooved stones used to weight fishing nets have been found, suggesting that the people caught and ate fish as well.

Though several sources of obsidian have been found along common travel routes, one near Teton Pass was the most popular. Obsidian Cliff in Yellowstone National Park was used as well as sites on Fish Creek near the foot of Teton Pass, a site at Bear Gulch in what is now Targhee National Forest west of the Tetons, and two other sites just east of the north end of Jackson Lake, one at Grassy Lake and the other near Conant Pass.

Major trails went up Owl and Berry Creeks and Webb Canyon in the north end of the Teton Range. Others went up Pacific Creek, the Buffalo Fork, the Gros Ventre and Hoback Rivers, and over Teton Pass. Because of the short growing season, the large mammals

migrated out of the valley to warmer, dryer areas at lower elevations, and the Paleo-Indians followed them from their summer base
camps. The Sheepeater Indians of Greater Yellowstone prehistory
were a Shoshonean people related to the Utes, Paiutes, Bannocks,
Comanches, and eastern Shoshones. Other tribes that traversed the
area on hunting forays and trade missions include the Bannocks,
Blackfeet, Crows, Flatheads, Gros Ventre, Nez Perce, and Shoshone.

Native Americans and the Snake

Shoshone

The Snake River's name derives from the Plains Indian sign language gesture for Shoshone, the peoples inhabiting the area when
the first Europeans arrived. Trappers interpreted the sign—the right
hand with thumb extended up, waving away from the body in a
snakelike motion—as "snake." Some historians believe, however,
that the Indians may have been indicating a pattern in the grass bas-
kets the Shoshone wove rather than the sinuous river along which
they lived.

In 1805, at the mouth of the Clearwater River in western Idaho,
explorers Meriwether Lewis and William Clark named the Snake
River the Lewis River. The two towns that eventually grew up at
this confluence became Lewiston, Idaho, and Clarkston, Washington, on opposites sides of the Snake. The Lewis appellation for the
river, however, survived only along a small tributary of its uppermost reaches flowing from Shoshone Lake to Lewis Lake, then out
of Lewis Lake in Yellowstone National Park to enter the Snake less
than a mile from the park's south entrance.

Interestingly, the sign for Comanche, a closely related tribe that
lived and hunted on the southern plains (in Texas, Oklahoma,
Kansas, eastern Colorado, and New Mexico), is similar to the
"snaking" sign that applies to the Shoshone. Instead of a hand
movement away from the body, the sign for Comanche is a weaving
movement toward the body (backward snakes). The Shoshones considered the Comanches a backward offshoot of their tribe, though
once the Comanches obtained the horse they became the greatest
horsemen of the southern plains. Before the coming of white men,
the Shoshones were the most frequent hunters in the Snake River
Valley. Shoshone words have been used to name several specific features of the upper valley and the Teton Range: Teewinot (many pin-
nacles), Shoshoko Falls (falling water), Lake Taminah (a spring), and

Togwotee (lance thrower, named for a Sheepeater guide who was proficient at a Shoshone game).

There are two present-day Shoshone reservations. The Wind River Indian Reservation lies east of Jackson Hole across Togwotee Pass on the Wind River near Dubois. The Fort Hall Indian Reservation, shared by the Shoshone and Bannock Indians, lies on the Blackfoot River in Idaho, a tributary of the Snake southwest of Jackson Hole.

The most famous Shoshone was Sacajawea, "bird woman" of the Lewis and Clark Expedition, who served the famous explorers of the northern Louisiana Territory as translator and a representative of goodwill, but not, as many historians have suggested, as the expedition's guide. The presence of a woman with a baby helped convince the tribes through whose territory the party traveled that the expedition was peaceful in intent.

Sacajawea also verified the party's location when the expedition entered Shoshone country, recognizing Beaverhead Rock for which the Beaverhead River in Montana is named. It was pure happenstance that the Shoshone band Lewis and Clark first encountered was led by her brother, though they were certainly traveling through Sacajawea's homeland.

Crows

The present Crow Indian Reservation lies in Montana just north of the Wyoming border, but traditionally the Crows hunted the headwaters of the Snake. Mountain men had found them generally friendly and occasionally wintered with them and took Crow women as wives. The first exploration parties in Yellowstone reportedly had positive encounters with the Crow people. But as European settlers pushed other tribes west—the Lakota, Cheyenne, and Arapahoe—the displaced tribes encroached upon Crow country, which was the primary reason the Crows fought on the side of the army in the battles of the Rosebud and the Little Bighorn. The Little Bighorn battlefield lies on the Crow Reservation.

Bannocks

The Bannocks were placed on a reservation with their traditional enemies, the Shoshones, near Blackfoot, Idaho, in the 1870s.

One of the saddest stories involving this tribe occurred in the summer of 1895. A small party of Bannocks (nine men with their women and children), starving on the ill-supplied reservation, visited their traditional hunting ground for deer and elk—a foray permitted and guaranteed by their 1868 treaty rights. Having followed the Snake River tributary, the Hoback, to Battle Mountain, they were attacked by a party of twenty-six Jackson Hole settlers who detained and disarmed the Bannocks. In the skirmish, one elderly Bannock was killed, a younger brave wounded, and a child abandoned as the families scattered. The child, held by Jackson Hole residents for several months, was ultimately returned to his mother. Newspapers all over the country headlined the Indian uprising, basing their stories largely on rumors. In the end, the Indians were denied their treaty rights, a position that was upheld by Wyoming's governor in a United States Supreme Court case that set the precedent of states' jurisdiction over wildlife.

Nez Perce

During the 1877 Nez Perce War, forced upon the nontreaty bands of the Nez Perce in northeastern Oregon and western Idaho, Chief Joseph tried to lead his people to safety in Canada. Finding their normal route to the buffalo plains of northern Montana blocked by soldiers and armed civilians, they detoured through Yellowstone National Park, which had been established only five years before. Entering near West Yellowstone, they crossed the park, following Nez Perce Creek (named after the war), and moved over rugged country to the east of the park, through Clarks Fork Canyon. The tribe attacked two parties of tourists during their trek through Yellowstone, killing one man and capturing several others, although Chief Joseph protected and released the tourists.

The Nez Perce were captured only a few miles south of Canada in the Bearpaw Mountains of northern Montana, a long way from their homeland, becoming part of the history of the first U.S. national park and of the Snake River headwaters.

The Laubins

Longtime residents of Jackson Hole, Reginald and Gladys Laubin devoted their lives and artistic talents to an intimate study of Native Americans and to the preservation and interpretation of their cultures. The two met at Norwich Art School in New England and eventually moved west where they immersed themselves in what would become their lives' passion.

For nearly twenty years—in the 1930s and 1940s—the couple lived

The breathtaking skyline of the Teton peaks is echoed by the tipis erected in the Laubin campsite. The Snake River flows in the middle distance, delineated by the line of trees along the river. The Laubins' "square tipi" appears at the far right. Courtesy of the Laubin Collection

with elders of the Lakota tribe on the Standing Rock Reservation in South Dakota and with the Crows in Montana, learning the Lakota language and many Indian dances. Together they wrote three books—*The Indian Tipi* (1957), *Indian Dances of North America* (1977), and *American Indian Archery* (1980)—about the Plains Indians at the height of the buffalo culture. The University of Oklahoma's Foundation of Indian Art and Culture also produced a series of documentary films featuring the Laubins in 1960 and again in 1983 to help preserve the wealth of Indian lore that they had gleaned through their relationships with native peoples.

Their best-selling tipi book, published the year I met them selling tickets to their performances at Jackson Lake Lodge, is dedicated "to the Plains Indians in the hope that their young people will recapture a pride of race, a love of color and beauty, and an appreciation of the good things in their own great heritage—today the heritage of all Americans." Their "square tipi," as Gladys called their log cabin, is located on Antelope Flats at the foot of a glacial terrace. They used to joke about their outhouse "with the best view in the world," which was fitted with a set of Dutch doors so that the upper half could remain open to the Snake and the towering Tetons beyond. For many summers—from the late

Reg Laubin dances the chief's dance he learned from One Bull, who fought in the Battle of the Little Bighorn. Courtesy of the Laubin Collection.

1940s until the early 1980s—the Laubins lived in an authentic tipi erected next to their cabin where they hosted many guests, Indian and non-Indian.

Reg, who called himself Black Buffalo and had a lone black buffalo head painted on his shield, was adopted by One Bull *(Tatanka Wanjila),* a nephew of Sitting Bull *(Tatanka Yotanka).* When writer Walter Campbell (Stanley Vestel), author of *Sitting Bull: Champion of the Sioux,* who is buried at the national cemetery at the Little Bighorn battlefield, introduced the old Lakota warrior to Reg, One Bull pointed to Reg's shield and said, "Look, he has my name."

One Bull was twenty-three when he fought at the Little Bighorn. He taught Reg the chief's dance as he had danced it the night of the infamous battle, counting coup, imitating the buffalo bull, growling like a grizzly bear in his anger at Custer and his soldiers. Reg was probably the first white man to know who killed Custer (probably One Bull's brother, White Bull) and how he died, for he heard the first-person accounts of the battle many times from the Lakota elders.

Gladys, too, was adopted into the One Bull family by One Bull's wife, Scarlet Whirlwind, and given the name Good Feather *(Wi'yaka Wastewin).* When Reg performed the chief's dance, she would interpret the sign language Reg used and assume the role of the good squaw. In addition to their appearances at Jackson Lake Lodge, the Laubins performed Plains Indian dances before the crown heads of Europe and Africa, from Finland to North Africa, and on the stage at Carnegie Hall.

In 1972 they won the prestigious Capezio Award for their artistic contribution to Native American dance, and four years later they were awarded the Catlin Peace Pipe by the Indian Lore Association, "For preservation and interpretation of Indian dance and culture."

The Early Explorers and Mountain Men

Shortly after the Lewis and Clark Expedition of 1804–1806, Spanish entrepreneur Manuel Lisa hired John Colter to get word to the various nearby tribes that Lisa had established a trading post at the mouth of the Bighorn River (known in its upper reaches as the Wind River). Colter had been a member of the Lewis and Clark party but took early retirement from the Corps of Discovery in order to remain in the western mountains. He wandered through the Yellowstone country the winter of 1807-1808. No one knows for certain if he entered the Snake River drainage or saw the Snake. Although shreds of evidence suggest that he did and that he even snowshoed through Jackson Hole that winter, his route has been subject to much conjecture and debate. Nevertheless, he is generally credited with its discovery, and certainly his stories of the region soon led other trappers into the high country surrounding the headwaters of the Snake River.

Colter's Hell, which several early historians placed in the Yellowstone geyser basins, almost certainly lay on the Shoshone River east of Yellowstone near present-day Cody, Wyoming. Colter's race for life against a band of Blackfoot Indians in the Three-Forks Country of the Upper Missouri is a popular story that fascinates devotees of the legendary mountain men, and it frequently appears in works of early fur-trapping days. Whatever Colter's role may have been in opening this country to the white man, the Upper Snake soon became a major crossroad of the Rocky Mountain fur trade.

Before returning home to a more genteel life in Missouri, Colter joined Manuel Lisa's fur brigade in 1808. The Lisa company included Andrew Henry, who established a fort west of the Tetons on what is to this day known as Henry's Fork of the Snake (occasionally called the North Fork). Henry, who advertised in a St. Louis newspaper in 1822 for trappers to go to the headwaters of the Missouri, is generally credited with starting the rush to the northern Rockies that led to the brief ascendancy of the "mountain man," which spanned the years 1824 to 1836.

Three of Henry's companions—John Hoback, Jacob Reznor, and Edward Robinson—trapped beavers in Jackson Hole in 1811. On their way east from Henry's Fork, they encountered Wilson Price Hunt's Astorians, an overland party sent west by John Jacob Astor to establish a trading post at the mouth of the Columbia River near where Lewis and Clark spent the winter of 1805–1806. A second prong of the Astorian party had sailed around Cape Horn to the mouth of the Columbia to actually build the fort.

The trio of trappers became guides for the Astorians, leading them down the Snake tributary that now bears Hoback's name, and into the lower end of Jackson Hole and the Upper Snake River Canyon. They camped at the location of today's Astoria Hot Springs, a few miles downstream from the mouth of Hoback River and a few miles upstream from the Grand Canyon of the Snake.

With forty French river men and only a handful of fur-trapping partners, the group tried building dugout canoes but found poor timber and rough water. "La maudite rivière enragée," they called the Snake: the accursed mad river. Friendly Shoshone Indians ultimately led the Astorians out of Jackson Hole over Teton Pass, but the Astorians, split into four groups, had a difficult time reaching their destination on the Columbia.

For the next few years Astorians and Canadians trapped and explored the Snake headwaters, but Jackson Hole did not get its name until the 1820s. To the mountain men a "hole" was a mountain-rimmed valley. The hole of the Upper Snake became a favorite haunt for David E. Jackson, who first arrived there as early as 1825, certainly by 1826. The Kentucky-born entrepreneur did not do much beaver trapping; he did not like to get his feet wet. Instead, he kept records for the fur company he purchased in partnership with Jedediah Smith and Bill Sublette on July 18, 1926, from William Ashley. Sublette is credited with calling the valley Jackson's Hole for his fur company partner.

Osbourne Russell's *Journal of a Trapper, 1834-1843,* documents this mountain man's journey west in the spring of 1834 with New England entrepreneur Nathaniel J. Wyeth in a party that included noted naturalist Thomas Nuttall (for whom are named Nuttall's woodpecker and Nuttall's goldenweed) and John Kirk Townsend (for whom are named Townsend's solitaire and warbler, and the wild-flower *Townsendia*). Once in the mountains Russell joined Jim Bridger's brigade and subsequently trapped throughout the drainage of the Upper Snake many times during his nine-year meanderings between the Yellowstone country and the Great Salt Lake. According to Russell, the abundant wildlife in the Jackson Hole area kept the men fed, spectacular scenery kept them fascinated, and encounters with hostile Indians kept life interesting. The trapping heyday had passed, but the legends would live on in the literature of western history.

In 1860 Jim Bridger led Capt. W. F. Raynolds's railroad reconnaissance party through the hole, and a few miners trickled in during the early part of the Civil War, from 1861 to 1862, attracted by gold rushes in Montana and Idaho. The Langford-Washburn party, accompanied by Lt. Gustavus C. Doane, explored the Yellowstone area, including part of the Upper Snake River drainage, during the late summer of 1870.

The Hayden Geological Survey party explored the Yellowstone area in 1871, including the Upper Snake. Richard "Beaver Dick" Leigh, a local guide for the party, settled on the west side of the Tetons, but frequently hunted and guided parties through the hole and supplied specimens to the Smithsonian Institution for many years until his death in 1899. Leigh Lake at the southeast foot of Mount Moran is named for Beaver Dick, and nearby Jenny Lake at the mouth of Cascade Canyon is named for his Shoshone Indian wife, who died of smallpox along with all their children during Christmas week, 1876. The Muries' book about their life in Jackson Hole, *Wapiti Wilderness,* reprints Leigh's letter telling the sad story.

The Hayden party turned to Jackson Hole and the Teton Range the following summer, in 1872, naming several features after members of the party: Mount Leidy for Joseph Leidy, Bradley Lake for Frank H. Bradley, Taggart Lake for W. R. Taggart, and Phelps Lake for George H. Phelps (a hunter of the region). Artist Thomas Moran, for whom Mount Moran is named, never actually visited Jackson Hole, but he did visit the Yellowstone area, made famous in part by his sketches and paintings. Pioneer photographer William Henry Jackson, for whom Mount Jackson at the southeastern corner of the hole is named, served the 1872 Hayden Survey team and made the first photographs of the area.

Robert W. Righter's *Teton County Anthology,* a collection of historical writings pertaining to the Jackson Hole area, includes "The Ascent of Mt. Hayden," Nathaniel Langford's account of his 1872 climb of the Grand Teton, known for a short period by a select few as Mount Hayden. Many doubt that the group successfully climbed the Grand, and Billy Owens, who definitely climbed it in 1898, led a lifelong effort to discredit the 1872 climb. However, historian and longtime resident of Jackson Hole Lorraine G. Bonney wrote a well-researched book in defense of the Langford claim, *The Grand Controversy* (1992).

Moran's sketches and paintings and Jackson's photographs of the Yellowstone area on the 1871 Hayden Survey, coupled with Doane's journal of the 1870 exploration of the Yellowstone area, had helped convince Congress to establish Yellowstone as the nation's—and the world's—first national park in 1872. In the late fall and winter of 1876 Doane led a more extensive exploration of the Upper Snake River country.

Although it was generally believed that this latter exploration promised little in the way of new information about the Snake River, no one had ever explored it in anything approaching a scientific manner. Doane hoped to study the region as a piece, fitting it into the larger story of the West, as Maj. John Wesley Powell had done on the Green and Colorado Rivers a few years earlier. Unfortunately, the elements and bad luck conspired against him. He and his men were fortunate to escape with their lives.

Doane's 1876 Expedition

Autumn came early that year to the Yellowstone high country. The aspens turned by early September, the cottonwoods along the rivers not much later. The woods rang with elk bugling, and beavers began cutting their winter food supply in dead earnest. An early snowfall sent ducks, geese, and sandhill cranes flying south. Even the grizzly bears, sensing something unseasonal, began raiding squirrel caches for pine nuts and seeking den sites. Indian summer followed with cold, crisp nights, clear, frosty mornings, and bright, lovely days full of sunshine and autumn color. The cottonwoods along the rivers and the aspens in the high country seemed to exude their own light.

Making the best of the fair weather, Lt. Gustavus C. Doane of the Second Cavalry reveled in his new assignment, one that he had earned not by soldiering but by politicking. His orders, directly from Gen. Alfred Terry but ultimately from Phil Sheridan, said in part, "Lt. G.C. Doane is ordered to make exploration of Snake River from Yellowstone Lake to

Columbia River." He was given a noncommissioned officer, five men, pack animals, and sixty days' rations, plus a boat that had been built to Doane's specifications and then disassembled for transport to Yellowstone Lake. Only sixty days to travel more than a thousand miles!

Doane's commanding officer, Maj. James S. Brisbin, had not been happy about this expedition nor about Doane's constant attempts to get special assignments that had little to do with chasing and corralling Indians. Doane was an adventurer by nature, full of ideas for exploring western rivers, distant mountain ranges, even the arctic regions and the Nile River.

This expedition, for example—exploring the Snake River from source to mouth—promised little in the way of new information. Its various segments were fairly well known. Lewis and Clark had followed its lower reaches in 1805-1806. (They had named it the Lewis River, but the name never stuck, except for the uppermost regions they never saw.) The Astorians had followed it for miles in 1811-1812, even venturing into Hells Canyon, and the mountain men had swarmed over it during the following decades, until the price of beaver dropped out of sight in the late 1830s. The Oregon Trail, in use since the early 1840s, followed the Snake for hundreds of miles. There was not much new to learn about the Snake.

Yet Doane was a persistent, if frustrated, explorer. He had wanted to venture down the Green and Colorado Rivers, but Maj. John Wesley Powell had beaten him to it. It rankled Doane that Powell still carried his military title but, having been discharged from the army, no longer had to put up with bucking the chain of command or with military protocol. Doane, on the other hand, had not been able to get military leave to explore the West as Capt. Benjamin Bonneville had in 1831.

Doane did not lack credentials for the enterprise he sought to undertake. He had entered the University of the Pacific as a science major, enrolling in all the heavy math and science courses, from astronomy and calculus to zoology and trigonometry. He had graduated with honors in classics, studying Latin and Greek. He served in the Civil War with the California One Hundred, rose from the ranks to a commission as first lieutenant, and served with the Marine Brigade (the original "horse marines") on the Mississippi.

As far as field experience in the northern Rockies, he had led the Yellowstone Expedition of 1870, commonly called the Washburn-Doane Expedition, the first attempt to explore the area of canyons, falls, lakes, and thermal phenomena known as Colter's Hell. He had even served as guide for the Hayden Survey parties of 1871 and 1872. He knew the Yellowstone region as well as any man—better, perhaps, than Jim

Bridger himself—and certainly as well as Nat Langford, the Yellowstone National Park superintendent, sitting in a post Doane coveted.

For all his disappointments, Doane loved being in those wild lands, especially when he was not under orders to fight Indians. His heart simply was not in the Indian wars. He admired the Indians and enjoyed his contact with the Crows as chief of army scouts at Fort Ellis. He was learning their language, their hand signs, and their customs. As an officer with General Terry's command that arrived at the Little Bighorn battlefield the day after Custer's defeat, Doane had devised a mule-drawn litter, patterned after an Indian device, for evacuating the wounded survivors of Reno's and Benteen's troops to the steamboat *Far West* on the Yellowstone River not far away.

He found a tipi to be a better home than any tent the military used: lightweight, portable, cool in summer, warm in winter, an ideal bivouac shelter. In fact, he had one along on this trip. He would have liked to have a couple of the young Crow warriors along as well. They knew the country better than he did. They understood the spirit of the land and had learned to live with it, using its power to sustain them and to enhance their lives. Doane felt something of this same kinship with Yellowstone's high country. He liked the weather and the elevation—and he certainly could not be expected to chase Indians there, not through the snows blanketing the land from October to April, anyway.

The Yellowstone country was full of wonders, full of wildlife, full of strange geologic phenomena such as geysers and hot springs, petrified forests and lava layers. It was wonderful to be back. Less than a week from Fort Ellis in Montana Territory, Doane and his men had entered the park October 16, leaving the discipline of military life behind. Some of the men had been with Doane before and knew the relaxed routine of his wilderness travel.

The Snake River rose across the Continental Divide from Yellowstone Lake, but Doane's plan was simple enough. He would rebuild the prefabricated boat on the lakeshore, caulk and test it there, have mules drag it over the snow to the top of the divide, then carefully slide it down the other side to Heart Lake, which Doane considered the source of the Snake. From Heart Lake he intended to follow the Snake to the Columbia.

The weather seemed to change as soon as the party entered the park proper. Indian summer ended with a sleet storm that night. The next day they moved on under gloomy and threatening skies that brought snow by midmorning. They camped on Tower Creek just above the falls, moving on the next morning through eighteen inches of fresh snow. It began snowing again during the day and continued on and off for several days. Finally, nearly two weeks after leaving Fort Ellis, they reached Yellowstone Lake and camped at its outlet on October 23.

On October 24 the party, according to Doane's journal, "prepar[ed] the outfit for the double transportation by land and water." They laid out the boards on the snow to absorb moisture so they could be more easily bent, and they cut and peeled tipi poles and raised the tipi for the first time. All the next day, in fine weather, they refitted the pack outfits and worked on the boat, caulking it with oakum and pine pitch from the surrounding forest. Late that day, "[Daniel] Starr and [F. R.] Applegate, both expert boatmen, paddled the little canoe far out on the sparkling waters and sang Crow Indian war songs." Yellowstone Lake had not yet frozen, nor would it while the Doane party remained in its basin.

They camped on the lakeshore for three days, working on the boat and testing it on the lake, swamping it once. The rest of the time they explored, fished, and hunted. According to Doane, they killed a deer and a goose, and "[m]urdered a lot of pelicans."

On October 28 the party split. Doane led most of the men with supplies and equipment around the West Thumb of Yellowstone Lake overland by horseback and pack mule, while Privates Starr, Applegate, and John L. Ward recaulked the boat and prepared to cross the lake. Doane would establish a campsite to receive the boaters the following day on what he called "the southwest arm where the foothills come on the shore . . . at the foot of the Great Divide at the nearest point opposite Heart Lake."

Doane and his horseback party then broke trail through two feet of snow to the top of the Continental Divide, where they surprised a grizzly bear, which ran away before they could get a shot at it. They crossed over to the Snake River drainage, again breaking trail, and camped in a hot spring basin above Heart Lake.

The next morning, October 30, Doane realized they had taken the long way around and broke a new, shorter trail back to the lakeside camp to find that the boat party had not arrived. At dusk, he ordered a watch fire built on a bluff above the lake to serve as a beacon to those in the boat. He grew worried; this was the third day, and "[a] wintry blast was driving down the lake in a direction at right angles to their course. The waves were running high." It grew colder as darkness descended, and a driving sleet began falling.

Certain that the men who, Doane wrote, had to navigate twenty miles "in an egg shell boat which had never been tried in rough water" would start no later than that night, he paced the shore, keeping the fire ablaze through his frigid vigil. "[S]uddenly there was borne to us on the driving blast the sound of boisterous and double-jointed profanity. The voice was Starr's and we knew that the daring invincible men were safe and successful."

Their oars were coated an inch thick with ice, and the boat, half full of solid ice from waves breaking into the open boat, was too heavy to bring ashore until the ice was chopped out with an ax. The men "were a sight to behold. Their hair and beards were frozen to their caps and overcoats and they were sheeted with glistening ice from head to foot." They spent the rest of the night thawing and drying out their clothes.

October 31 was sunny and bright. Using the mules, the men began dragging the boat over the divide, a task that took four days. No longer needing the extra men, Doane sent Ward and Morgan Osborn back to Fort Ellis with their horses and three of the exhausted mules. (Ward and Osborn had their own difficulties getting back, but that is another story.) Doane and his party had the boat, seven horses, and four pack mules. They had been on the trail for three weeks.

After drying the boat over a bed of coals, they recaulked it with pine pitch and "stripped her bottom with split poles of green pine." They raised the tipi for the first time in the Pacific watershed and feasted on duck and porcupine as they reworked the boat.

On November 6 they loaded their gear into the boat, launched it on Heart Lake, and headed for its outlet, the Snake River—and disappointment. Finding the lower end of the lake iced over, they once again used the mules to drag the heavily laden boat to the outlet, which they found only fifteen feet wide and six inches deep, not enough to float the craft. Their first day on the river they covered only three miles, hauling the boat by hand down a canyon that fell two hundred feet in less than a half mile. The second day they "[w]orked hard all day dragging the boat over rocks in a channel where she would not float at any point. Used a mule part of the time, and wore out the bottom of the boat as well as ourselves making three miles. Abandoned one horse and one mule."

The winter conditions continued to prevail in this high country of the Upper Snake. Temperatures dropped so low that water leaking into the boat froze, effectively caulking the seams—until Doane and his men ran across hot springs, which melted the ice, forcing them to stop, dry out the boat, and recaulk it. They did not reach the Lewis River until November 18. Doane called it "the true Snake River," though elsewhere in his journal he gives the Heart Lake outlet, now known as Barlow Creek, that credit.

The song of a black ouzel, which Doane called a water canary, cheered them briefly. Their painfully slow progress and their inability to

At the confluence of the Lewis and Snake Rivers. The Doane party camped in the meadow across the Snake to dry and recaulk their boats during the November 1876 exploration of the Upper Snake. Photo by Verne Huser.

find game in the snowbound landscape had sapped their energy and taxed their food supplies. "The problem was to get where the boat could carry the property and make distance before the animals gave out. Also to get to settlements before rations were exhausted." The lighthearted expedition of a few weeks earlier had become an ordeal of survival. November 23, the day the party reached Jackson Lake, the men tried eating one of the abundant river otters, but all became ill from the fishy flesh. The next day they ate their last flour. Warren, the fisherman, kept them well supplied with trout, thin fare for hungry, hardworking men in arctic conditions.

Finally, on November 25 they killed their first deer since October 26. As it swam in the lake, they fired at it twice with a twelve-pound Sharps buffalo rifle, creating a reverberating echo from the Teton Range. "The report of the big rifle was followed by a prolonged roar that seemed to eddy in the little bay in a vast volume of condensed thunder, then charged up the great glacier channel in a hollow deep growl giving consecutive reports which bounded from cliff to cliff and these re-echoed until far up the canon came back a rattle of musketry as on a skirmish line, mingled with mournful waves of vibratory rumbling. . . . Time, one minute and 26 seconds."

As the party worked its way along the longer western shore of Jackson Lake, they abandoned horses and mules worn out by too much work and too little fodder. The men, too, had health problems: Doane and Sergeant Server, too ill to travel, delayed the party, which reached the outlet November 29, its fiftieth day. On November 30 they found the river for the first time "large enough to float the boat with everything in it."

They made good time through Jackson Hole (the area now preserved as Grand Teton National Park), covering up to thirty miles a day by boat, but were reduced to eating their horses.

They met an old trapper living in Jackson Hole, John Pierce, who gave them a shoulder quarter of elk, which they consumed on the spot. He also gave them detailed information on the nearest settlement downriver, a mining camp several miles up a tributary creek. It was information that would ultimately save their lives. The party "worked on down the river with renewed strength among rocks and tortuous channels."

December 9, their sixtieth day, found them struggling through "rolling cascades [in which the boat] danced like a duck through the boiling surges. . . . We had a most exciting day and made 10 miles."

The river was open with an ice foot, as Doane called it, along either bank, a thin ledge of ice at the water's edge on both sides. This ice foot would erode where the current played against it, providing uncertain, slippery footing for the men maneuvering the boat. The party remained split, some traveling with the boat, others on horseback or on foot along "mountain sheep trails."

Where the current slowed, the ice foot might extend across the entire width of the river, creating an ice bridge, another hazard for the craft. On December 10 they "[f]ound the river in bad order. The gorge had torn away the icefoot and ice was massed in the eddies grinding and crunching in a very ominous way." Below they found the river consisted of "frozen pools and boiling rapids." Their food was gone now except for "a handful of flour. Shot White's horse, and feasted."

They endured their worst experience on December 12: "The River was becoming better, the ice foot more uniform and the channel free from frozen pools when all of a sudden the boat touched the margin, turned under it, and the next instant was dancing end over end in the swift bold current. All of the horse meat, all the property, arms, instruments and note books were in the roaring stream." They salvaged whatever floated—their tipi canvas, bedding, and bundles of clothing—but now they were essentially destitute.

They traveled on foot for more than three days without food or any means of acquiring it in temperatures between ten and forty degrees below zero. Finally, on December 18 they reached the mining commu-

In the Snake River Canyon. The Doane party found rough boating in the Snake River Canyon in midwinter, alternating between fast water and ice bridges. The "ice foot" along the bank is obvious in this photo. Photo by Verne Huser.

nity of Keenan City, in what is today extreme eastern Idaho above Palisades Reservoir. There they were fed and spent several days recuperating.

The day after Christmas, while Doane and his men struggled toward Fort Hall, bent on continuing their expedition, they were met by Lt. Joseph Hall of the Fourteenth Infantry with a small party of men sent to arrest Doane and his men as deserters. Their sixty days were up, and Doane's Major Brisbin, still miffed by the whole idea of the expedition, was retaliating.

Brisbin had put an ad in a Montana newspaper offering "$30 each for apprehension and capture" of Doane and his men. Nonplussed at finding the Doane party, Hall placed himself and his men at Doane's disposal and all had a hearty laugh. Doane said Hall, postadjutant at Fort Hall, denounced Brisbin "in unmeasured terms and told me that I was being made a victim of infamous treachery."

Doane intended to continue the trip. He wired Brisbin on January 4, 1877, from Fort Hall, saying, "Arrived here today. All well. . . . Will refit and proceed at leisure." Brisbin did not reply directly, but on January 8 the commanding officer of Fort Hall received a telegram, dated January 6, from the adjutant general in Chicago, saying, "You will direct Lieut. Doane . . . with his escort to rejoin his proper station Fort Ellis, as soon as practicable." Brisbin had wired General Terry of Doane's losses of military equipment, horses, and mules, and recommended that Doane be ordered back to his post.

Doane's Snake River expedition, a failure by most standards, added an interesting chapter to the history of the Yellowstone–Jackson Hole area, now largely protected as national park- and forestlands. His experience would help earn him the command of this country's first polar expedition in 1880. Though no men were lost, that expedition also failed, through no fault of Doane's. It would, however, lay the foundation for later and more successful exploration.

A few months after the unsuccessful Snake River expedition, Doane found himself once again in the park, trying to stop Chief Joseph and his Nez Perce refugees from escaping to Canada. Just as he moved into position to block the Indians' movement through the park, where they had already attacked two parties of tourists, he was ordered to wait. The Indians escaped, prolonging the Nez Perce War another month and costing dozens of lives, both Nez Perce and military.

Doane, who wanted more than anything else to become superintendent of Yellowstone National Park, never realized that dream. Battered and badgered by the military, he nevertheless served a vital role in the exploration of the northern Rockies. His name lives on in two minor northwest Wyoming peaks, one in Yellowstone National Park and the other in the northern Teton Range in Grand Teton National Park, but he was no minor character in the exploration of the region.

Prospectors and Preservationists

In 1886, during the prospect-mining days on the Upper Snake and a decade after Doane's ill-fated expedition in 1876, the first recorded murder occurred in Jackson Hole—a triple killing at what has come to be called Deadman's Bar. Three Germans panning the river's glacial gravels for gold—Henry Welter, T. H. Tiggerman, and August Kellenberger—ran out of supplies. When they traveled to Idaho where they had contacts, seeking to resupply, they found a young German immigrant, John Tonnar, with enough money for a grubstake. The trio took him in as a partner and soon began making his life miserable, working him to weariness, beating him on a regular basis, and generally encouraging him to abandon the partnership—now that they had spent his money.

Nursing his bruises and his resentment, the young German killed all three of his nefarious mentors, leaving their bodies half-buried under rocks in a sluiceway. The crime might have gone undetected for months, even years, but a survey party negotiated that stretch of river a few weeks later and discovered the remains of the three miners.

The young killer, found working on a ranch in Idaho, was arrested, tried, and acquitted on grounds of self-defense—there being no eyewitness accounts and nothing but circumstantial evidence. Tonnar soon disappeared, slain, perhaps, by friends of the murdered men or frightened out of the area by threats to his life. The debate continues among historians whether the bodies were found on the right bank of the Snake above the modern river access or on the left bank near the Lodge Company's lunch area.

Fritiof Fryxell, an early park ranger who visited the site forty-two years after the incident in 1928, published an account in *Annals of Wyoming* describing the location as "on the north side of the Snake in the SW1/4 of Sec. 23, T44N, R115W." Fryxell actually found the sluiceway and several prospect pits.

The few miners who visited Jackson Hole from time to time found only flour gold that was hardly worth panning. Mormon farmers and aspiring cattlemen began to appear in the valley to raise grain and to reap the hay growing naturally in several parts of the valley that had fattened elk for centuries. Why not livestock as well? The first settlers came in 1884; by 1889 the population of the valley had grown to sixty-five. In 1890, when Wyoming became a state, Jackson Hole had fewer than one hundred residents, but even then tourists had begun visiting the valley. In 1884 George Bird Grinnell, editor of *Field and Stream,* visited northern Jackson Hole on a Yellowstone trip. Theodore Roosevelt, who became president in 1901, hunted the Teton Wilderness in 1892. Englishman Sir Rose Lambert Price, who married Eliza Osgood Vanderbilt, hunted in Jackson Hole in 1898.

In 1892 Bill Menor became the first settler west of the Snake. He began farming and then opened a store, but most of his potential customers lived east of the river. In 1894, after a careful survey of the Snake, he established a ferry in the vicinity of present-day Moose at the one place where the river runs in a single channel and is accessible from both sides.

Powered by the river, the ferry was attached by a rope to each end of a board that ran on sheaves along a cable across the Snake. The rope was attached to the ferry, running through a capstan, by means of which the angle of the ferry to the current could be altered. As the current caught the angled ferry, it moved the craft across the

Menor's Ferry in 1918 with Blacktail Butte in the background. Courtesy U.S. Forest Service.

river. When the angle of the ferry was brought parallel to the current, the force of the water became equalized, and the craft stopped moving laterally. Reversing the craft was merely a matter of reversing its angle relative to the current.

Menor soon learned, however, that the ferry could not be used in high water. During one spring flood a huge tree, drifting in the flow, collided with the ferry, breaking it away from its cable. The ferry came to rest on a gravel bar a few hundred feet downstream. Menor's neighbors helped him haul the heavy craft back upstream, where he repaired the damage and continued operating.

Menor ran the ferry from 1894 until 1918, charging fifty cents for a team and wagon, twenty-five cents for a rider on horseback; all other passengers rode free as long as there were paying passengers on board. He sold out to Maud Noble, who doubled Menor's prices and operated the ferry until 1927 when the first bridge built across the Snake in the middle valley put her out of the transportation business.

The new bridge served the area until 1957, when the modern bridge was completed. A historical restoration project in 1949, spearheaded by Harold P. and Josephine C. Fabian and financed by Laurence S. Rockefeller, rebuilt Menor's Ferry. This replica, operated by National Park Service volunteers, still crosses the river as a visitor service during the summer if water conditions are favorable and safe.

A small town grew at the ferry crossing. Menor's brother Holiday joined him in 1895 and operated a lime kiln on the east bank of the Snake, using limestone from nearby Blacktail Butte. Apparently, the Menor brothers did not get along well—one reason they lived on opposite sides of the Snake. Both were prone to using profanity, and locals reportedly could not tell which of the brothers was the meaner of the two.

In the 1920s Jack Dornan homesteaded on the east bank just south of Holiday's lime kiln and married the local schoolmarm, Ellen Jones, in the first wedding at the newly built Chapel of the Transfiguration. Ellen Dornan continues to greet morning visitors to Dornans' chuckwagon breakfast served in two tipis on the left bank of the Snake directly across from the Moose river access, where most scenic float-in-the-park trips terminate.

The 1920s brought increasing interest in preserving this corner of the Old West among local residents and the occasional visitors to the valley at the foot of the Tetons. Author Owen Wister, who had first visited the valley in 1885, set part of *The Virginian* (1902) in Jackson Hole and began writing about the area. Struthers Burt, who owned and operated the Bar B C Ranch where Owens stayed during his visits, began to publicize the area, establishing one of the first dude ranches in the valley.

Severe winters in 1909, 1910, and 1911 brought to public attention the effect of human habitation on natural processes in the Jackson Hole area. Forced to winter in the valley after civilization blocked their migration routes to the Red Desert, the elk population began plummeting. Jackson Hole writer and photographer Stephen N. Leek documented the plight of the starving elk herds. His compelling photographs, along with the efforts of local ranchers and the Wyoming State Legislature, ultimately led to the national-level recognition that was required to save the elk. An act of Congress of August 10, 1912, established the core of what would become the National Elk Refuge. Over the years presidential executive orders, further acts of Congress, and private donations initiated by the Izaak Walton League of America added to the elk refuge, which now comprises almost twenty-five thousand acres devoted to wintering wapiti and other wildlife species.

This initial conservation victory spurred other preservation efforts, as did reaction to exploitative activities in several corners of Jackson Hole. As early as the 1890s a few farsighted residents had begun discussing the expansion of Yellowstone National Park to the south to preserve Jackson Hole and the Tetons. Beginning in 1918 Congress considered a series of bills aimed at protecting these areas, but Idaho reclamation forces, politicians, and their rural constituents who used Snake River water for irrigation proved too powerful a lobby.

Stephen Leek's photographs documented the effects of human habitation on the migration of elk herds in Jackson Hole. His work led to the establishment of the National Elk Refuge. Courtesy of the Jackson Hole Historical Society.

By the 1920s more serious efforts had begun toward staving off commercial exploitation. An important meeting took place July 26, 1923, in Maud Noble's cabin on the Snake. Struthers Burt, Horace Carncross, Jack Eynon, Joe Jones, and Dick Winger met with Yellowstone superintendent Horace Albright to outline a proposal for preserving the area.

In 1926 Albright gave John D. Rockefeller Jr. and his family a tour of Jackson Hole and soon won a pledge from the wealthy philanthropist to help preserve the area. Beginning in 1927 the Snake River Land Company, a Utah-based corporation, began using Rockefeller money to purchase private property in Jackson Hole. At the time, few knew that the purchases were aimed toward preservation. At a Senate subcommittee public hearing in Jackson Hole in July 1928, seventy-six of seventy-seven participants supported protection for the Teton Range. In 1929 an act of Congress carved Grand Teton National Park from the Teton Forest Preserve. It included only the east face of the Teton Range from Webb Canyon in the north to Granite Canyon in the south and a few of the piedmont lakes, but not Jackson Lake or the Snake River.

Maud Noble's cabin near Menor's Ferry in Moose where a pro-park group met in 1923 to plan conservation strategy. Photo by Verne Huser.

Rockefeller interests continued to purchase private lands in Jackson Hole even as the park began to function against growing opposition. The Forest Service had fought the park idea for decades, and local opposition to park protection for the valley began to grow, spurred by local ranchers who feared losing free grazing rights. In another public hearing in 1938 local residents voted 162 to 3 against park expansion.

Bills in Congress to expand the park had failed in 1933 and again in 1938. Rockefeller's patience began to thin. He wanted to give the nearly thirty-three thousand acres of land he had purchased for the preservation of the Upper Snake River Valley to the people of the United States, but the people of Jackson Hole and their representatives seemed to want nothing to do with preservation.

Then, on March 15, 1943, with a stroke of Franklin D. Roosevelt's presidential pen on Executive Order 2578, the valley lands purchased by Rockefeller money—consolidated as Jackson Hole Preserve, Inc.—along with Jackson Lake and additional forest lands, became Jackson Hole National Monument. The action set off a firestorm of protest and vilification in Wyoming.

Several weeks later, in a well-orchestrated publicity stunt, armed ranchers on horseback led by movie actor Wallace Berry "invaded" the new Jackson Hole National Monument to generate national interest in what they considered a local travesty. When the Forest Service turned over their existing facilities to the National Park Service, they trashed the buildings, removing all furniture, even the plumbing. Lawsuits were filed, and congressional bills were introduced to abolish the monument.

It required seven more years of political bickering before the establishment on September 14, 1950, of a new, expanded Grand Teton National Park, incorporating the national monument lands, including additional forest lands, and protecting many miles of the Snake River and its adjacent wetlands.[1]

1. For a more detailed and highly readable account of the history of protection for the Tetons and the valley known as Jackson Hole, see Robert W. Righter's *Crucible for Conservation: The Struggle for Grand Teton National Park* (1982). Currently out of print, the book is bound to be republished; it is too valuable not to be available to the general public. Righter's 1990 collection of local writing, *A Teton County Anthology*, remains available; it includes some interesting local writings of historical significance: accounts of the early visits to Jackson Hole by Owen Wister and George Bird Grinnell, by Wister's eleven-year-old daughter, Fannie, and by Ernest Thompson Seaton's wife, Grace Gallatin Seton-Thompson, describing fording the Snake River in a covered wagon, Theodore Roosevelt's 1892 elk hunt on Two-Ocean Pass, and Stephen Leek's "Starving Elk of Wyoming," one of the pieces that ultimately led to the establishment of the National Elk Refuge.

A story worth mentioning here concerns Maggie Corse and the Bar B C Ranch, once owned and operated by Struthers Burt. The owner of the ranch when the national park was first established in 1929 had sold out to the Park Service in 1933 with the common stipulation at the time that he and his wife could live on the land tax-free and rent-free for the rest of their lives. His wife died, and after a few years the husband married Maggie; then he died. Maggie, fairly young at the time, became owner-with-lifetime-lease. She clung to the Bar B C in a most serious manner: she hunted ducks and geese along her section of river and fished where and when she damn well pleased, despite seasons and limits. She ruled the place like a queen, and the rangers were scared of her. More than fifty years after her late husband had sold out to the park, Maggie died (August 3, 1988), and the Park Service finally had use of the historic property, though they have not had the budget to do much with it. Budget constraints have also prevented the park from hiring a resident historian.

During World War II help had been hard to find, and a couple of winters Maggie had no one to shovel the snow off the cabin roofs. The weight broke their backs and their ridgepoles, and many of them have not been the same since.

Maggie put little effort into maintenance during her latter years, and the place began to fall apart. The Park Service has not had the budget, since acquiring the property, to renovate the cabins, which naturally continue to deteriorate. The Jackson Hole Historical Society has surveyed the situation, raised some funds, reroofed some of the buildings, and generally tried to preserve the historic structures, but it seems to be a losing battle against the elements--and congressional budgets.

Floating the Snake

For a half century following the Doane expedition of 1876-1877, few people negotiated the Snake River. A handful of surveying parties and a few dozen fishermen occasionally plied its pristine waters. In 1909 gold prospector Ivan Hoffer ran the canyon in a boat controlled with ropes from shore, a decidedly dangerous activity. Because of severe flooding during spring snowmelt runoff and poor understanding of the river's hydraulics in general, few people ventured onto the river. Recreational activity was minimal. Most people were afraid of the Snake and with good cause, given the crafts available and the level of boating skills. Famed river runner Amos Burg is reported to have run the canyon in the mid-1920s in a small inflatable raft, and Don Smith of the Salmon River in Idaho ran the Snake in a wooden scow manned with sweeps in the mid-1940s.

As early as 1936 Dick Barker's stepfather, Joe Beerkle, guided fishing trips on the Snake for Bob Carmichael, who ran a tackle shop and general store in Moose near Menor's Ferry. Bob was the fishing concessionaire for the park, and he and his wife lived in Maud Noble's cabin. In those days the main highway crossed the Snake on the bridge built in 1927 just south of the Menor's Ferry site (the cut is still visible through the shoreside vegetation, and a small riffle on the river results from what is left of the old bridge pilings). At low water a few fingers of ancient rebar still stick up, obstacles to navigation.

During World War II Carmichael purchased hard-hulled Penn-yanes, special boats used for fishing the river, but fishermen did not engage in much float fishing in those days, although they used the boats to get from place to place for shore fishing.

Shortly after the war, though, the traffic on the Snake increased significantly. The Craighead brothers, John and Frank, began fishing the Snake on a regular basis in small inflatables, and Boots Allen began offering commercial fishing trips. Over the next ten years, foldboats and kayaks came into use. In the summer of 1956, the Grand Teton Lodge Company began offering scenic float trips.

Raymond Lilly is credited with the idea of running trips-for-hire for the public. He, along with park superintendent Frank Oberhansley and Boots Allen, explored the twenty-two-mile Pacific Creek–to–Moose segment of the Snake and then began taking passengers on board.

After a minor accident on the Bump Stump (a name we will discuss later), Butch Pope began managing the lodge's float trip

A busy day on the Snake River at the canyon launch site.
Photo by Verne Huser.

operation, guiding trips himself that summer through 1958. Frank Ewing broke in as a guide in 1957, my first year as a trainee guide. By 1959 the float business was booming. Only the Grand Teton Lodge Company sold scenic float trips to the general public at the time, although a handful of guides offered fishing trips and a few guest ranches offered both scenic and fishing trips. The Lodge Company had what amounted to a monopoly on the Snake between the late 1950s and early 1960s.

Then a number of individuals, observing the explosion in scenic float trips and the monopoly that the Lodge Company enjoyed, challenged the company's right as prime concessionaire to be the sole provider of services on the river. They won without a fight: in 1962 the National Park Service issued special-use permits to several new river outfitters.

The number of outfitters doubled, then tripled each year until, at the height of the explosion in the late 1960s, there were nearly fifty.

Veteran river guide Al Klagge, who holds the record for most miles logged—
45,110 as of September 2000—guiding on the Snake River.
Photo by Verne Huser.

Many of the operations left something to be desired in safety and
visitor service, hiring teenagers off the streets of Jackson Hole to become overnight guides. In 1970 park superintendent Howard Chapman warned the outfitters that if they did not begin to control themselves, the Park Service would have to start managing the river and
control its use. Nothing changed.

The National Park Service then began to limit the number of people on the river; the situation had gotten completely out of hand.
They began to control boating on the Snake, based on historical use:
first by limiting the number of outfitters to whom they issued permits, then by limiting the number of boats each outfitter could
launch on a given day, in a given season. The Park Service also
began to require guides to have Red Cross first-aid certification and
to take an interpretative course from park naturalists before they
could be licensed to guide on the Snake. The number of approved
river outfitters was eighteen, but consolidation and attrition has reduced that number, though not the overall traffic.

By the early 1970s several outfitters had begun offering commercial whitewater trips in the Snake River Canyon. There were initially no restrictions or limits, then an informal voluntary monitor-
ing system. In the fall of 1973 the Forest Service entered the river
management business seriously and began limiting each outfitter to
the number of boats run during the 1972 season.

River running on the Snake in Jackson Hole has become big business, but more and more private boaters, using a wide variety of rafts, canoes, kayaks, and dories now ply the Snake's braided channels and whitewater. Commercial use has begun to level off with roughly one hundred thousand people floating the scenic stretch through the park, and another hundred thousand testing the canyon whitewater every year.

New generations of river runners continue to make history on the Snake River, and the old stories get better every year. The big floods of 1996 and 1997 were not as high as the one in 1943, according to river denizen Bob Dornan, but they refashioned the river in many places.

A number of the guides I know who have watched the river change through the decades speculate that if it shifts west toward the base of the mountains, the Snake will find a course along an ancient channel that cuts through the woods west of the 4 Lazy F Ranch and through the Park Service headquarters, where a recently expanded maintenance building now blocks the view of the Tetons for floaters as they leave the river at Moose Landing.

Barker-Ewing and the Snake River Model

In the early days of river floating, the watercraft generally used on the Snake were military surplus boats—bridge pontoons, assault boats, life rafts—a wide variety of crafts not specifically designed for river use, but serviceable nonetheless. The advent of a boat specifically created for floating was several years away, still hidden in the imaginations of two enterprising figures of Snake River history.

Dick Barker grew up in Jackson Hole and spent summers at his grandfather's log house on Ditch Creek. He had been a Snake River fishing guide for Carmichael's Tackle Shop in Moose as early as 1956. Frank Ewing, in contrast, was a newcomer to the river valley who had grown up in Kentucky and studied botany at Yale. Frank was just passing through Jackson Hole in the mid-1950s on his way to Alaska when he discovered the Tetons and the Snake River; he liked what he had found, got a construction job, and in 1957 began guiding scenic float trips for the Grand Teton Lodge Company.

In 1963 Frank and Dick each started his own scenic float trip company, providing Grand Teton National Park visitors with a more intimate river experience by using smaller boats and running shorter trips

The Snake River model has become so popular that it is used from the Potomac River on the East Coast to the Olympic Peninsula on the West. Courtesy of Demaree Inflatable Boats, Inc.

on the shoulders of the day, early mornings and late afternoons. Their wives, Barbara Barker and Patty Ewing, were part of the family business, baking brownies and cookies and fixing cider and lemonade for passengers on the river. They drove shuttles and occasionally did some guiding themselves.

In the fall of 1965 Dick and Frank, friends and competitors, turned their collective knowledge of river running to designing a boat that would become the craft of choice on the river. They created on paper a boat that they thought would best serve their purposes: a boat that would keep people dry on the scenic section, offer maximum passenger-carrying capacity, safely negotiate the river's fast current and numerous shifting channels, and be relatively easy to operate. Their plans culminated in the Snake River model, two prototypes of which were built by Rubber Fabricators in West Virginia in time for the 1966 season.

When Rubber Fabricators sold out to one of the major rubber companies, a new company, Rubber Crafters, began making the same models and hired Dave Demaree, an experienced river runner as well as a good businessman, to market the company's products. Demaree, who now has his own company, Demaree Inflatable Boats, still makes the Snake River models.

Dick and Frank entered a limited partnership, Barker-Ewing, for the 1967 season and purchased a third Snake River model, which sold for roughly one thousand dollars. As business boomed, they began to sell their boats to other outfitters, who were anxious to find good boats. Surplus rafts were aging; they were scarce, expensive, and when they could be obtained often leaked both air and water.

In 1972 Barker-Ewing purchased seventeen Snake River model boats, kept eight for their own operation, and sold the rest, including several to the Grand Teton Lodge Company. That same year, the partners began offering whitewater trips in the Snake River Canyon, and a decade or so later Dick and Frank divided the original business with Dick operating scenic trips in the park and Frank running the whitewater trips in the canyon.

The Snake River model became so popular that the enterprise went international: Frank and Patty Ewing, on vacation in New Zealand, scheduled a float trip with a rafting company that not only used Snake River boats but also had copied the Barker-Ewing brochure to the extent of using a picture of the Snake River with the Tetons in the background on the cover. Today Barker-Ewing-designed Snake River models remain the boats of choice on the scenic stretch of the Snake in the park, while a variety of other crafts appear on canyon whitewater, many of them manufactured by Demaree.

The Tradition of River Names

Names for specific points along the river came into being over time as people who knew the Snake well—and in the early days of river floating, they were primarily the guides for the Grand Teton Lodge Company—applied logical names to obvious features or sightings: the Oxbow Bend, the mouths of tributary streams (Polecat Creek, Pacific Creek, Buffalo Fork, Spread Creek, three Cottonwood Creeks, Gros Ventre River, and Hoback Junction), Teton Marsh, the Elbow, the Narrows, Fence Rapid, and Rope Rapid. Other names pertain to human inhabitants and activities: Flagg Canyon, Cattlemen's Bridge, RKO Camp (where *The Big Sky* was filmed), Deadman's Bar, Schwabacher Channel and Landing, Bar B C Channel, 4 Lazy F Channel, Wilson Bridge, South Park Landing, and Astoria Hot Springs.

In recent times many features on the river were named by boatmen who applied an intimate knowledge of the river and its wildlife toward a standardized nomenclature that all boatmen would recognize. Guiding float trips for the Grand Teton Lodge

Fence Rapid. An underwater ledge system creates one of the first rapids in the Snake River Canyon. Photo by Verne Huser.

Company in 1959, Frank Ewing and I normally captained different boats. After a day on the river, we would compare notes:

"How many moose did you see today?"

"Six."

"Where did you see them? We only saw three."

"Well, we saw the old bull with the crooked antler on that island just above where the river starts to spread out—you know, where you can first see the Triangle X Ranch."

"Yeah, we saw him too. But after lunch we only saw two big bulls on the right just above Cottonwood. Where were the others?"

"The other five—three bulls, a cow, and a calf—were all on that big island below the Bar B C Ranch. You know where the river funnels into that narrow chute and the river splits around a big island?"

But even with these time-consuming exchanges of information we could not be sure we were talking about the same locations, so we began naming river segments and features: the island where the crooked-antlered bull often fed became Bull Moose Island, and the area just below that, where the river began to split into several channels, became the Spread. The Funnel disappeared with channel changes long ago. Many Moose Island became Not-So-Many-Moose Island when moose populations declined, and in the summer of 1996 we often called it Mule Deer Island because we saw deer there

Rope Rapid lies just below the huge pool below Lunch Counter Rapid in the Snake River Canyon. Photo by Verne Huser.

nearly every trip. Last Chance Island and Channel grew out of a sense that this was where boatmen and passengers would have their last chance to see any moose at all.

Naming features along the river became a kind of game, but a majority of the active guides had to agree on an appropriate name. The Buffalo Channels were obvious: the silt carried by Buffalo Fork created a series of islands just below its mouth. The deep, fast, narrow channel with the overhanging spruce tree became Spruce Ditch.

The area where springs entered the river from the Elk Ranch irrigation overflow became known as Spring Bank Bend. The bend where the bank swallows nested became Bank Swallow Bend; another higher cut bank where bank swallows also nested became Swallow Bank, but was also known as Lone Spruce for the single spruce tree that grew immediately above it, and occasionally as Eagle's Perch, for one of a pair of bald eagles that nested in the heavy timber on the right bank and almost always perched in the lone spruce on the left bank. We could spot the bird a half mile away.

When Walt Disney photographers filmed a documentary on the Snake, we boatmen named the bank where they did most of their filming the Disney Bank, and the channel that at high water entered the heavily forested shoreline on the right just above, the Disney Channel. Another area several miles downstream was named Otter Bank because in filming *One Day on Teton Marsh,* the Disney crew released two otter-actors there, then dumped a truckload of river cobble over the edge of the cut bank to simulate a landslide called for in the script. The trained otters never came back; apparently, they liked Snake River trout better than their Disney salaries of old fish.

According to Dick Barker, Disney offered a hundred-dollar reward for the otters' capture. As the story goes, guide Dick Dornan was fishing a gravel bar downstream just above Menor's Ferry several weeks later when one of the semitame otters began harassing him, even swimming between his legs. Dick threw rocks at the otter to frighten it away, only later learning that he had just chased away a big bounty.

Names changed as the channels themselves changed or as other events became associated with particular locations. According to Dick Barker, what was originally known to locals as the Air Strip—for a landing area that actor Wallace Berry had bulldozed out of the sagebrush flats near his cabin on Jackson Lake—became RKO Camp when the studio began making movies in the vicinity. Later, the riverbank known as RKO Landing—because it offered a boat take-out—became Fisherman's Camp because so many fishermen drove the RKO Road to fish the Snake. It remained Fisherman's Camp even after the Park Service closed the area to camping in order to enhance the wildlife habitat.

As more and more river outfitters began to operate on the Snake, guides for various companies began using different names as well. Once the Park Service developed a river management plan, river rangers appeared to enforce the regulations. Most of the early rangers worked closely with guides and outfitters who knew the river well; some later river rangers did not, arbitrarily applying meaningless names to various sections of the river—a pattern that created problems.

Once, for example, a canoe wrapped around the head of an island we boatmen called Spruce Divide because a huge spruce tree had lodged for years on the upstream point of the island. Traditional guides radioed the Park Service to report the accident, but the Park Service did not know Spruce Divide because the new rangers had not learned the old names and had applied different names that the guides did not know. A serious misunderstanding ensued that delayed rescue efforts. In recent years, however, the Park Service, working with guides and outfitters, has attempted to standardize river nomenclature in the interest of safety.

Spruce Divide has seen its share of accidents. Jim Elder wanted to call it Matricide Point after he dumped his mother-in-law into the Snake at this point during a private family trip. A kayaker drowned there a few years later when his craft nosed under the log and the force of the current pinned the paddler underwater. Spruce Divide suggested names for channels below the divide: Spruce Divide Right and Spruce Divide Left. The name has survived even though the log itself has long since gone downriver with high water; flood years rearrange the furniture of the river in a remarkable manner.

A channel that flows through Schwabacher Island has a sad story behind it. Hamburger Channel is named for Dr. Hamburger, a fisherman whose body was found in the river there. Several miles upstream at the Triangle X picnic area, he had stepped into a hole too deep for his waders, which filled with water. When he sank, the current swept him to his death and temporary resting place. He had been a longtime Triangle X guest.

We named the Bump Stump in 1959 after an event involving a Grand Teton Lodge Company float trip in the summer of 1956. The two guys who initially operated the big pontoons with sweeps fore and aft could not decide who was boss; they were partners. One day in a moment of indecision, neither willing to tell the other what to do, they hit the snag anchored securely to the bottom of the river, and three paying Lodge Company passengers fell into the swift current, bumped off by the impact.

Wet and cold, they were dragged back into the craft, no worse for their experience, but that night the guides were called on the carpet by Lodge Company management and asked to explain. They stood together as a team, refusing to determine who would be boss, and were both fired on the spot. Butch Pope, on Bob Koedt's recommendation, became the new river boss, and he ran a clean, safe river-trip operation for the several years he remained at the helm.

With that story always in the back of our minds, experienced boatmen avoided the Bump Stump, which at that time lay near the left bank two and one-half miles below the Lodge Company's lunch stop near Deadman's Bar. It was not difficult to miss, but in the summer of 1959 a big pontoon operated for guests of a dude ranch hit the Bump Stump dead center and everyone on board went for a swim, guides and guests alike. The pontoon's metal frame wrapped around the Bump Stump and hung there for two or three days. There were many pictures taken of the wreck, to the chagrin of the dude rancher, whose company name, emblazoned in red paint, was obvious from certain angles.

In the early days of Snake River float trips only two pairs of bald eagles nested along the twenty miles of river we ran each day. We referred to them as the morning eagles and the afternoon eagles because we stopped for lunch between the two nest sites; we called them the Morning Eagle Nest and the Afternoon Eagle Nest. Several of the names we applied to sections of the river related to the eagles' presence and patterns: Eagle's Nest Channel, Eagle's Rest Channel, the Eagle Tree for favorite perching sites, and Eaglets' Perch, an arched root on which the just-fledged eaglets liked to rest from their strenuous activity of first flight.

When the bald eagle nest tree blew down in the summer of 1973 and the eagles built a new nest across the river from the old one, we debated whether to change the name of Eagle's Rest to Eagle's Nest, but history prevailed: the right channel is still Eagle's Nest even though the last several nests have been on the left (Eagle's Rest) channel. When beavers, who had a lodge on the bank below one nest tree used in the early 1990s, cut down that nest tree, we named the small channel that flowed past it Lost Nest Channel.

Two narrow, shallow channels that ran into the right bank just above the old eagle's nest, both initiated as beaver canals, we named the Forest Channels because they led right into the woods. Only at high water levels could they be run and then only by experienced guides, but they offered excellent wildlife: ducks and ducklings, bison, occasional moose, often elk. Line Camp Channel, named for an old line-camp cabin on the right bank (long since removed by the Park Service to destroy the last visage of the cattle-industry past and to allow the area to revert to a wilder state), flowed to the right below the Forest Channels. It gave us opportunities to see elk, bison, eagles, moose, deer, and fishermen, and get a closeup view of a beaver lodge and a patch of special wildflowers known as elephantheads.

A hundred yards below the Otter Bank two slots in the edge of the outwash plain allow floaters to see the Teton peaks one by one, passing in review as they drift by the erosion cut, peeks of the peaks so to speak. We named the site Peekaboo Bend. The summer of 1996 a new channel opened immediately below Peekaboo Bend, a straight-shot high-water shortcut we had noticed for years but had never found enough water to run. We named it Peekaboo Street in honor of the American Olympic skier. Latter-day Lodge Company guides renamed Peekaboo Bend the Windows, and when the new channel opened nearby during that flood year, they called it Windows '96.

Deadend got its name when Maggie Corse, who owned the Bar B C Ranch, had her wranglers cut down a tree to block the channel to keep floaters from drifting past her guests' picnic area on the riverbank. Lodge Company guides who used the channel the next time down the river had to step ashore and drag the heavy pontoon a half mile upstream to get back on the river. The channel later opened up again when the next high water removed the tree, and it became a major channel for float trips as the river has shifted to the west. A huge cottonwood tree, scarred by years of beaver work at its base, fell into the river during the summer of 1996 as Maggie's picnic area began to crumble into the Snake. In late spring a garden of low larkspurs decorates, in a vivid deep purple, what remains of the picnic area.

The beavers blocked another channel just above Schwabacher Landing with similar results; that channel now bears the name Beaver Dam Channel. Nearby another high-water channel went dry as the river dropped, suggesting the name Lindburn's Dust Bowl when a guide by that name tried to negotiate it much too late in the season. Today, because hardly any of the present guides remember Lindburn, it is generally known simply as the Dust Bowl. Two backwaters on the Bar B C Channel where early Barker-Ewing trips stopped to serve cider and brownies on evening trips became Upper Cider Slough and Lower Cider Slough.

The summer Barker-Ewing began offering whitewater trips in the canyon, their guides, without guests, ran a dozen or more practice trips to get to know the river. On the evening before the first paying passengers were scheduled, the guides made one last run with their wives and girlfriends. The rising river offered serious rapids in a place or two, one of them a sharp hole with a steep wave immediately below a ridge of rock that the river had only partially cut through. Located just below the Blue Slide on U.S. 26/89, an area prone to landslides, it formed a vicious hydraulic.

The guides decided to go for the gusto, hit the hole and wave head-on, and were stopped dead in the water. Spun sideways and with three oars broken (two operational oars and one of the two spares), the self-bailing boat was forced into the hole time and time again, frigid water pouring into the boat and flowing out the bottom. The boat throbbed and cavorted; its passengers, wet and rapidly growing hypothermic, were terrified. After about eight minutes—though it seemed like hours—the river gods finally relented, spit the boat out of the hole, and the crew nursed the boat to shore in an eddy downstream, using their only remaining oar. They named the rapid the Three-Oar-Deal.

In 1967 Henry Tomingas and Dave Hansen, who were certainly among the first outfitters to make commercial trips through the canyon, ran an all-day private trip for one of the Diamonds, a group playing a gig at the Wort Hotel in Jackson. It was a Sunday; they had launched at Moose the night before—Dave, Henry, and Mike Douglas of the Diamonds and their girlfriends—and had camped on the island at the mouth of the Gros Ventre. They decided to go all the way to Palisades Reservoir.

As they entered the canyon, Dave and Henry realized the river had dropped since their most recent trip. Rounding the bend below Blind Canyon, they heard the roar of the rapid just above Lunch Counter, which had not been anything to worry about on this stretch two weeks before. They had just been drifting along most of the day, nursing their collective hangover, not expecting any problems. As they approached the growling, pounding rapid, Mike Douglas, who had just played in Hawaii, yelled, "Here comes the Big Kahuna." They hit the hole and flipped.

The meaning of *Kahuna* is often misconstrued, especially by casual visitors to the island paradise. Kahuna actually means a powerful priest or doctor, perhaps even a witch doctor who can do either good or evil—certainly an appropriate way to think about this rapid.

Lunch Counter Rapid was named by two intrepid guides, neither of whom had negotiated the whitewater rapids of the Snake River Canyon—and neither of whom would admit it. As they approached the biggest rapid in the canyon for the first time, the river called their bluff. The two looked at the tumbling waves and the huge holes and agreed that the rapid could very well flip their boat and eat them for lunch.

Denny Becker, one of the pioneer outfitters in the canyon, named one of the rapids Cottonwood because Cottonwood Creek enters the Snake in the midst of the rapid. Charlie Sands and John Simms called it Holy City because of its many holes. Dick Barker and Frank Ewing, fresh from their first trip through the Grand Canyon, a training run for Snake River whitewater, called it Little Sockdollager after a rapid on the Colorado. Finally, someone—the wit will remain nameless—suggested it be called Little Holy Cotton Sock to satisfy all parties. It is generally known as Cottonwood today.

Denny Becker named Champagne for its numerous bubbles caused by the constriction of the current through a deep, narrow slot. John Simms named Rope for its resemblance to a braided rope: waves breaking off the steep limestone cliffs on the left weave into waves breaking off the ledge on the right, forming a pattern that looks like a rope.

My own political leanings became apparent when I named a channel for Ronald Reagan: it was far to the right and rather shallow. A winding, bushy, high-water channel that runs through the Big Island is called Ping Pong because a boat in the channel bounces from bank to bank. Knowing a place well enough to name it suggests that a real bond exists between that place and person. Guides who have been on the river long enough to have named a rapid or two take a proprietary interest in *their* rapid; they never forget the stories of the rapid and the stretch of river immediately above and below it.

Bump Stump is the place that belongs to me in this way. I have watched this snag for more than forty years; it has not moved, but the river has. Once only 25 or 30 feet from the left bank—just enough room to sneak a pontoon between it and the left shore—the Bump Stump today lies more than 150 feet from that left shoreline near a midstream gravel island, proof of the manner in which the Snake River continues to change—and proof that there will always be new stories to tell about it. The tradition of river naming will go on, and, of course, so will the river itself, long after those of us who leave chosen names behind.

Geology of the
Upper Snake River Valley

The Upper Snake River flows through a region shaped by millions of years of continuous geological activity. Many of the results are not discernable to human observers, such as the fraction-of-an-inch-a-century rise of the Teton Range and the accompanying subsidence of Jackson Hole. But though the tectonic movement that builds mountains takes time, other geologic events occur rapidly and are more readily observed.

One segment of the Snake River lost 150 feet of bank during the twin flood years, 1996 and 1997, while the opposite bank gained 200 feet as gravel bars silted in and cottonwoods, seeded naturally in the newly deposited silt, began to grow, reclaiming land from the river. The river's main channel simply moved west a few dozen yards and narrowed slightly.

As rivers flow, they tend to meander, curving within a distance of five to seven times their width, making a complete double curve or S within ten to fourteen times their width. The current, normally stronger on the outside of the bend, cuts deeper there; on the inside of the bends, where the water slows, it drops its suspended load, and the water is shallower. Rivers change constantly with varying flow levels, especially during spring snowmelt, and wherever the current slows, suspended materials settle out. The river carries a heavy load.

This basic geologic process of erosion and deposition causes the river to range back and forth between its floodplain terraces like a gigantic earthworm that eats silt, sand, and gravel and deposits its waste in its wake. We should learn by observing such natural phenomena that rivers bound by artificial barriers such as dikes and levees will have their way with the land as the Mississippi River floods of the early 1990s and the El Nino floods of 1998 so dramatically illustrated.

Between mountain peak and riverbed other geologic forces are at work: weathering, frost heaving and frost wedging, plant- and animal-caused erosion, the annual cycle of winter snowfall and

Rivers meander through their floodplains, curving sinuously back and forth within a distance of five to seven times their width. This view, looking southwest from Blacktail Butte, shows the Snake River meandering through Jackson Hole. Photo by Verne Huser.

Constant deposition and erosion caused by a river creates braiding channels such as these below the mouth of Cottonwood Creek. Photo by Verne Huser.

Virtually the entire valley floor of Jackson Hole was deposited by glaciers. Here, below Deadman's Bar, the terraces created by the Snake River's cutting through the glacial moraine are obvious.
Photo by Verne Huser.

summer snowmelt runoff, and glaciation with its capacity to carve rock away from the peaks and carry it elsewhere, depositing its rock debris wherever the ice begins to melt or the glaciers begin to recede. Virtually the entire surface of the valley floor of Jackson Hole as we see it today was deposited by glaciers and turbulent rivers that resulted from the melting of glacial ice. The final sculpting of the Grand Teton mountain range as we see it was formed largely by glaciation.

The most significant long-term geologic factor of the Snake River landscape is the Teton Range itself. Essentially, the block of rock

The majesty of the Teton Range is captured in this historic panoramic photograph from the 1930s. Grand Teton is the tallest peak, with Mount Owen to its right and Teewinot below. These three peaks are also known as the Cathedral Group. Continuing from Grand Teton, right to left, are Middle Teton; a trio of peaks on the ridge that are South Teton, Cloud-veil Dome, and Nez Perce; the double summit of Mount Wister; pyramid-shaped Buck Mountain; and Static, the broad peak located just above a snow basin. Courtesy of U.S. Forest Service.

from which erosive forces have carved the range rose from the bowels of the earth in a massive uplift of ancient rock. Simultaneously, the valley floor sank. This *tectonic movement,* as geologists term the twin uplift and sinking action, began as early as 34 million years ago, and started to form as a Basin Range normal fault about 13 million years ago, a movement that continues through the present day.

One way to get to the bottom of things, geologically speaking, is to start at the top: the summits of the high Teton peaks, composed of ancient crystalline rock, began forming 2.8 billion years ago as sedimentary rock. Due to the depth of its burial and the heat and pressure generated at a depth of ten miles beneath the earth's surface, it altered or "metamorphosed" (literally, changed form). Molten rock beneath the earth's crust created much of that pressure, and in many places it actually fractured the subsurface layers, flowing into cracks and crevices, cooling and hardening there as intrusions of granite and other fire-formed rock. Pressure and heat altered adjacent rocks, which sometimes broke away to join the molten flow

Banded gneiss, a metamorphic rock, characterizes the core of the Teton Range. The banding is caused when ancient sedimentary layers are transformed by heat and pressure over geologic time. Metamorphic literally means "form changed." Photo by Verne Huser.

and become embedded in the matrix as zenoliths (from the Greek *zeno,* meaning foreign, and *lith,* meaning rock). Layered sediments became warped as they altered, leaving evidence of their distortion in cliff faces and boulders that weathered away from those cliff faces.

At times this whole subsurface regime lay beneath ancient seas that concreted sediments and served as a habitat for living creatures that captured chemicals from the saltwater and created limestone layers full of fossils. Many thousands of feet of alternating layers of sandstone, siltstone, conglomerate, and limestone formed beneath these ancient seas. Then the land rose, and the layers deposited beneath those ancient seas dried to become a solid cover of older sediments that had changed to become the metamorphic core of the Teton Range.

All this took place below the surface of a relatively level landscape more than 30 million years ago. Then the faulting began. In fact, it had probably been going on in a minor way for a long time before the Teton fault occurred, causing the mountain block to rise and the valley floor to drop along a sharp line, a crack that geologists call a fault. Both blocks tilted to the west, the mountain block rising and the adjacent valley block sinking.

What fuels these changes, forcing the blocks to move when and where they move? No one really knows, but most geologists believe

Fossilized crinoid stems in a limestone layer that once covered the Teton Range. Remnants of this deposit occur on the west slope of the range. Photo by Verne Huser.

that the engine generating the activity has something to do with the movement of molten magma eighty to ninety miles beneath the Yellowstone area, a huge volcanic system known as a hot spot. This hot spot probably created the regional uplift that helped pull apart a series of faults in the Basin Range province. Again, no one fully understands hot spots, but they constitute an important aspect of geologic activity.

Hot spots formed the Hawaiian Islands. As the Pacific plate drifted across a hot spot far beneath the Pacific Ocean floor, occasionally the hot spot burped up a release of magma that ascended to penetrate the surface. As the molten rock cooled and hardened, it became an island. The linear movement of the plate across the hot spot explains the chain of islands, known as a hot-spot track. There will be more burps and more islands—just as there will be more volcanic activity in the Yellowstone–Grand Teton region, where geologists have found evidence of three major volcanic eruptions followed by twenty-nine separate minor events.

The westward tilt of the mountain block led to gradual erosion toward the west and sudden, massive erosion to the east. Thus, the east slope of the range became precipitous, the west slope more moderate. The valley block, also tilted westward, gave a gradual westward slope to the valley floor, which began to fill with debris. During prehistory the Snake River flowed along the base of the

The mountain block from which the Teton Range was carved began rising and tilting more than 30 million years ago, while the adjacent valley block where Jackson Hole is today began sinking. The westward tilt of the Teton fault is obvious in this view from the high country. Photo by Verne Huser.

mountains, along the Teton fault, the lowest part of the valley floor at that time, but glacial debris from the Yellowstone plateau and from mountain block erosion in the Tetons began to build up in Jackson Hole, forcing the Snake away from the base of the mountain block that continues to rise along the Teton fault.

The opposite sides of the Teton fault slip slowly past each other, building tension that may be released suddenly and dramatically in an earthquake. I felt the 1959 Hebgen earthquake near the southwestern edge of Yellowstone National Park, which killed a number of people. I later visited the site and observed the massive destruction it had caused. As recently as the summer of 1997 evidence of the quake remained in the rubble below Hebgen Reservoir, created in part by the massive earthquake-generated landslide, similar to the 1925 Gros Ventre slide in Jackson Hole, which may have been triggered by a series of minor earthquakes in the valley.

The postglacial movement on the Teton-fault escarpment can be seen clearly above String Lake and from any vantage point that provides the visitor with a clear view of the shoulder of Rockchuck Peak above String Lake and of the lower northeast shoulder of

The town of Wilson during the 1927 flood, which occurred when the natural dam, created by the Gros Ventre slide in 1925, was breached.
Courtesy of U.S. Forest Service.

Teewinot. A marked depression along several hundred feet of mountain slope can be seen, especially in the afternoon when the angle of sunlight reaching this east-facing slope hits it just right: a thirty-eight-meter drop appears, indicating a slump at the fault line, clear evidence of the continuing movement of the Teton fault.

The erosion of the Teton Range and the filling of the valley with debris from that erosion constitute slow processes, but the Gros Ventre slide came suddenly. A wet spring in 1925 saturated a weak zone on the north end of Sheep Mountain, lubricating underlying shales to the extent that part of the mountain simply slid some two thousand vertical feet into the valley below. Fifty million cubic yards of material, more than was moved to dig the Panama Canal, slid into the valley of the Gros Ventre River in a matter of minutes. It dammed the river, forming a sizable impoundment, Lower Slide Lake. The scar on the mountain was a half-mile wide and a mile long; the lake created by the slide was two hundred feet deep, five miles long. Similar slides had occurred farther up the unstable Gros Ventre Valley from 1908 to 1912 to form Upper Slide Lake.

In mid-May 1927, another wet spring, the waters of Lower Slide Lake began to percolate through the natural slide that had dammed it. Although a few people worried, the Army Corps of Engineers

Glaciers carve U-shaped valleys as they advance and retreat. The Teton Glacier and the valley it has created are visible to the right of Grand Teton, the tallest peak in the Teton Range. Photo by Verne Huser.

pronounced the dam safe. But on May 18, 1927, the waters of Lower Slide Lake breached the natural dam, and much of it washed out in a catastrophic eight-foot wall of water and mud, creating a tremendous flash flood that drowned six people and destroyed the town of Kelly, the largest community in the valley at the time. The flood damage was evident all the way to Idaho.

The fact that flooding was also experienced in the town of Wilson on the far west side of the valley several miles away offers evidence that the valley floor does indeed tilt to the west. Fish Creek, which flows through Wilson and ultimately helped drain the floodwaters into the Snake several miles to the south, lies fifteen feet lower than the Snake River bed at the Wilson Bridge across the Snake.

During the Pleistocene Ice Age 1.6 million years ago, glaciers that existed worldwide receded during alternating periods of lower snowfall, warmer temperatures, and higher snowmelt; the Snake River's flow along the base of the range altered abruptly and significantly. The mountain glaciers that carved the canyons left debris dams at each canyon mouth, and the gigantic valley glacier that covered the floor of Jackson Hole by as much as two thousand vertical feet left debris dams across the valley floor, forcing the river eastward.

Bradley (left) and Taggart (right) Lakes lie at the foot of the Teton Range. These piedmont lakes were formed by glacial debris, known as a moraine, left by retreating canyon glaciers. Trees grow on these moraine dams where enough soil is formed from glacial till to support tree growth. Photo by Verne Huser.

The Snake had to find a new route through the outwash plain, a route well away from the fault line, far out into the valley. Over the centuries the valley filled to a depth of many thousands of feet with erosion and glacial debris, but while this deep deposition occurred the mountains were being ground down by these same forces, providing some of that debris.

The Teton fault has been measured at a displacement of twenty-four thousand to thirty thousand feet, but the offset between the valley floor and the mountaintop seems never to have been much greater than its present seven thousand feet. The various forces of erosion—weathering, frost wedging, rainfall and snowmelt runoff, glaciation, plus plant and animal activity—continued carving away at the mountain block, filling the valley floor with the debris and with material brought in from elsewhere by the massive valley glaciers.

However futile its efforts may be, the U.S. Army Corps of Engineers attempts to keep the river from flowing westward to lower elevations by building dikes and levees. Outside Grand Teton National Park these constrictions of the Snake River have, ironically, *created* floods because they restrict the river's natural attempt to spread into its floodplain. Since the 1940s when the Corps came to the valley, artificial dikes have been used to protect Wilson and other private properties lower than the river, but the river remains obstinate, seeking, as water must, the lowest point it can find.

The steepness of the east face of the Teton Range results directly from the Teton fault, the line between the mountain block and the valley block. Numerous small cross-faults have occurred, forcing the central part of the block higher than either the northern or the southern parts of the range. Thousands of feet of sedimentary layers eroded from the mountain block have left the high central peaks devoid of their sedimentary covering with the most prominent exception being Mount Moran, the northern-most of the high peaks. It has a sedimentary cap as well as an igneous intrusion formed by a thick vertical sheet of hardened magma, known as the black dike, which is about 1.5 million years old. The sedimentary cap can best be seen late in the summer when the summit snowfield has melted. Remnants of the sedimentary layers still overlay the northern, southern, and western parts of the range.

The black dike on Mount Moran, 150 feet wide near the summit, is composed of a diabase material, a dark igneous rock similar to basalt, a common surface rock in the region. A major climbing route, the CMC (for Chicago Mountaineering Club), on Mount Moran follows the black dike, which stands out in bold relief from the metamorphic mass of the mountain. In contrast, the black dike on the Middle Teton, composed of a more brittle material, appears as a chimney, twenty to forty feet wide, that rises vertically from the base of the mountain at the forks of Garnet Canyon and can be followed all the way to the summit, especially in late summer when most of the snow has melted from the peak's east face.

A third black dike, forty to sixty feet wide, on the southern ridge of the Grand Teton can be seen better from the west side of the range and by climbers on the peak itself, for the main access routes to the summit of the Grand Teton cross the dark band. In late summer when the snow melts it is also visible from the east, appearing between the southwest ridge of the Grand Teton and Tepee Pillar, named for a climber who died here.

So sheer is the east face of the range that its primary erosion channel, Cascade Creek, has actually cut deeply into the range, bisecting it. From Rockchuck Peak south to the South Teton, the north and south forks of Cascade Creek drain the western aspect of the high peaks, then join into the major east-flowing stream in the heart of the range to pour into Jenny Lake. The hydrographic divide of the range actually lies three to five miles west of the high peaks.

Streams flowing eastward off the northern part of the range flow into Jackson Lake and then into the Snake at the dam. From Mount Moran south to Rockchuck Peak streams flow into Leigh Lake, then by way of String Lake to Jenny Lake. Streams south of the South Teton all find their way into Fish Creek, which flows south for miles along the base of the Teton fault, entering the Snake in South Park, where a reverse fault tilts it toward the main river.

A Snake River float trip within the park drifts past the whole Teton range, giving passengers a panoramic view of the high central peaks from Mount Moran to Buck Mountain. Jenny Lake drains into the Snake by way of Cottonwood Creek a mile above Moose Village (park headquarters).

As the steep east face of the range presents itself to the sunrise and to Snake River floaters, so the western aspect of the Tetons slopes gently into Idaho where sunset shadows paint weird patterns on the high peaks, and colorful fields of wildflowers serve as appropriate foreground for more spectacular views of this magnificent range. West-slope streams flow into the Teton River, a major tributary of Henry's Fork of the Snake, and ultimately into the Snake itself at Idaho Falls.

Three major glacial episodes have dumped their debris in the valley of the Upper Snake River: 1) the Buffalo episode roughly 1.9 million years ago, involving a mass of ice estimated to have been more than a thousand cubic miles in extent, part of a worldwide ice age; 2) the Bull Lake episode perhaps fifty to eighty thousand years ago, composed of a smaller mass of ice that left substantial deposits of quartzite boulders in the valley, laying the base of modern Jackson Hole and scouring out the valley floor of all soil when it melted; and 3) the Pinedale episode, occurring during the past thirteen to fourteen thousand years. The latter event was the least extensive but the most recent and left the primary features of Jackson Hole as we know it today: the potholes, Timber Island, and the Burned Ridge moraine, among others. Together these glacial periods have helped carve the mountain range, scarred such valley features as Signal Mountain and Blacktail Butte, filled the valley with debris to a depth of many thousand feet, left moraines in several parts of the valley floor, and deposited glacial outwash plains.

Glacial outwash describes the debris dumped or deposited by receding glaciers. Like a combination of conveyor belts and bulldozers, glaciers move material, carrying or shoving rock, gravel, soil, silt, all kinds of debris they quarry from surrounding obstacles as

Glacial outwash does not provide adequate soil to nurture trees. One place trees can grow is in potholes, which appear as small islands in a sea of sagebrush here below the Burned Ridge moraine. Photo by Verne Huser.

well as debris that may land on the glaciers' surface as a result of avalanche or windblown dust. When the material consists of variously sized gradients that remain in a mix, it is called till and ultimately serves as soil. The fine materials in the mix may be carried away by the melting glacial water, leaving only large chunks of glacial debris, devoid of materials to form soil and hold surface water and nutrients necessary for plant growth. Glacial outwash plains, leveled by the turbulent, turbid streams that create them, have little ability to grow large plants, especially trees.

Most of the valley floor of Jackson Hole is covered so deeply in glacial outwash that trees will not grow there for lack of substantial soil and the water it holds that trees need to survive. Consequently, sagebrush and a highly limited association of grasses and forbs dominate. Trees do grow on the lower east-facing slopes of the Teton Range and wherever glacial till has provided soil: on the terminal moraines of the canyon glaciers at the base of the mountains, with piedmont lakes nestling in the moraine-formed hollow, and on the terminal, lateral, and medial moraines of a series of valley glaciers such as the Burned Ridge moraine and Timber Island.

Trees also grow in the potholes, commonly called "kettles" in New York and the Upper Midwest. Potholes result from the melting of huge chunks of glacial ice imbedded in the outwash. As the ice melts, depressions form, filled with meltwater. These small lakes ultimately fill in with windblown dust, vegetation, and other natural organic debris to form soil.

Viewing the Jackson Hole Valley

An ancestral Snake River has carved its course through the glacial outwash plain, diverted into a huge S-curve by the Burned Ridge moraine below the Snake River Overlook on the Eastside Highway (U.S. 26, 89, and 187). Driving north along this road a few miles north of Moose—between the Glacier View and Teton Point turnouts—a traveler can easily see the secondary river terraces formed by a much larger Snake River. At one place a tertiary terrace covered with young aspens indicates an ancient bend of the river. Trees also mark other ancestral river channels and bends.

The Snake River Overlook on the Eastside Highway offers a spectacular view of the Teton Range and a scenic segment of the Snake River, but it may help orient the visitor to some of the most obvious geologic patterns in the valley. Looking north, you notice that the outwash plain constituting the valley floor is two or three hundred feet lower than the outwash plain to the west or south. The lower level represents an earlier outwash plain, one that has been overridden by more recent glacial activity. This recent glacial activity dumped a new outwash plain on top of the earlier, older one at a lower level, beginning at this point.

From the overlook you can see the level, treeless plain of the valley floor; you can observe the various layers of outwash debris, leveled by the depositing river that resulted from the melting glacier; and you can see river terraces and bends of ancient water routes where no river exists today. From the well-placed Snake River Overlook, you can see the course of the Snake River through the outwash plain and identify its ancient channels. You can see numerous potholes to the northwest, north of the Burned Ridge moraine across the river. These depressions are now filled with lodgepole pines, the first trees to invade an area that has not previously supported trees. Driving north along U.S. 287, you will pass through an undulating area of more vegetation-filled potholes, including Hedrick's Pond, where trumpeter swans have nested on a beaver lodge. On the lower level, you can see two or three more pothole ponds to the right of the highway on the east side of the valley.

Looking toward the Teton Range from the overlook, you will see the Burned Ridge moraine across the river, another area where trees grow on the material left by receding glaciers. You can also observe the river terraces at different levels. Immediately below the overlook, you can look down at the Grand Teton Lodge Company's meal site and see old river channels marked by aspens and lodgepole pines that grow where these prehistoric streams deposited enough silt to hold enough moisture to grow trees.

Another impressive site for viewing the geology of the valley floor and the Snake River is Signal Mountain, which has a road to its summit. Two viewpoints besides the summit itself offer views of the valley: one at Jackson Point Overlook on the southwestern aspect, and the other, Emma Matilda Overlook, to the north, overlooking the Oxbow, Cattlemen's Bridge, and the Snake's loop around the north end of Signal Mountain. You can also see two depressions in the glacial moraine where Two Ocean Lake and Emma Matilda Lake lie. Jackson Lake Lodge is visible on the back of the glacial debris ridge.

To see the Teton Range, Jackson Lake, and the potholes, walk a hundred yards on a paved trail from the Jackson Point Overlook parking area to an overlook facing southwest. The entire range and the valley floor appear as a life-size map lying at your feet. From here you can see the pattern of sharp topography created by the Teton fault: Teton Range rising steeply from valley floor, mountain glaciation (sharply carved peaks, living glaciers, U-shaped canyons, terminal moraines marking unseen but obvious piedmont lakes at canyon mouths), as well as the outwash plain with its special features (potholes, moraines, terraces) and the course of the Snake River as it turns to the southwest, its preferred direction.

From the summit of Signal Mountain the view is to the east and southeast: the Snake River's loop around the north end of Signal Mountain (the confluence of Buffalo Fork with the Snake is largely hidden), ancient dry-channel courses, Cow Lake, the old RKO Road, and the Snake River's course all the way to Blacktail Butte and beyond.

All of these elevated viewpoints will help you see the general geologic patterns: the erosion of one bank and the deposition on the other, the various plant succession patterns that depend upon geological activity, the undercutting of the bank, the filling of channel mouths, and the deposition of silt on the bank during high-water episodes.

Floating *through* the landscape offers, however, a more intimate experience, one that scenic overlooks simply cannot. Nothing can compete with the sound of sand and silt whispering against the bottom of a boat or canoe or the feeling of a current tugging a craft downstream.

Archie Teater

A few hours before I was to report for my first day of work in Jackson Hole in June 1957, some friends and I turned off the highway to Jackson Lake Lodge and saw an artist sitting under an umbrella by a beaver pond, painting a scene of the Tetons.

He turned to us with a smile and asked, "Park savages?" using the term for college students who work summers in national parks. We excused ourselves for intruding on his painting, but he waved our apology away as though it were a mosquito and continued chatting with us as he worked. The Snake and its associated beaver ponds and tributaries were often the subject matter of Archie's paintings, but it was not only his artistic vision of the natural world that was instructive. Much of the oral history of Jackson Hole I learned from Archie, who pulled no punches in telling what he knew about the town of Jackson and its many colorful inhabitants.

Orphaned at sixteen, Archie had supported himself by panning gold along the Snake River in southern Idaho. By the time he turned nineteen he was building trails in the nearby national forests, and at twenty-two he owned a string of horses and had begun taking dudes into the Sawtooth Mountains. When Grand Teton National Park was created in 1929 just as the Great Depression began, he hired on as a member of the park trail crew. During the winters he attended art school in Portland, spending his summers working on Teton trails. He painted in his free time and sold his work by leaning it against his tent at Jenny Lake Campground with a price tag on each painting. By the time I met him, he was a well-established artist, a specialist on Teton landscapes—and eventually of mountain scenery around the world.

Both Archie and his wife, Pat, are gone now, but I cannot drive by their old cabin on Cache Street in Jackson without thinking of them, and whenever I look at the Tetons, I see Archie's rendition of the towering peaks. A few local galleries may still have a Teater or two, and Jack-

Painter Archie Teater at work in the summer of 1973.
Courtesy of the Teater Family.

son Drug Store on the northwest corner of the town square still displays
some of Archie's work—including a painting of the town square with
Archie's self-portrait in the lower right-hand corner, flashing his sparkling
eyes and displaying his mischievous smile.

PAUL M. MUIR 1979

Snake River Plant Life

Trees and Shrubs

Trees along the Snake River in Jackson Hole, both deciduous and coniferous, are the largest and most obvious plants. Blue spruce, which may not seem as blue as Colorado blue spruce but are nonetheless a member of that climax species (a final-stage species, a member of a mature forest community), dominate the older riverbanks. A few scattered, ancient cottonwoods, another climax species, grow among shoreline spruce, but wherever the river comes near enough to the old giants to offer the beaver an opportunity to cut them for food, the cottonwoods soon succumb to this mammal's appetite. The river dispatches both species when it undercuts the banks in its annual spring flood.

Plant succession patterns along the Snake differ from those of the higher river benches, the moraines, or the mountain slopes. On the river the willows colonize first, followed by cottonwood, both narrow and broadleaf. The narrow-leaf variety constitutes the most common deciduous tree along the living river. The willow-cottonwood forest provides the shade and wind protection that allows the major conifers to get started. They, in turn, ultimately outgrow the deciduous trees to dominate the climax forest, which may include spruce, Douglas fir, subalpine fir, and a few isolated limber pines, usually higher up on the cut banks, especially along the Burned Ridge moraine. A few limber pines live at river level at the Bar B C Ranch and others at the 4 Lazy F Ranch.

Spruce trees have sharp, stiff needles that appear square in cross-section; fir trees have flat, flexible needles, blunt on the end. Alliteration serves as a reminder: fir needles are flat and flexible; spruce needles are sharp, stiff, and square in cross-section. Douglas fir trees, whose scientific name means "false hemlock," have large fir-like needles, but their cones give them away: Douglas fir cones hang down. Cones of true firs stand upright on the bough when mature and disintegrate there, releasing their seeds and scattering them from the treetops, leaving center spikes, or "candles," standing upright after the cones fall apart, the remnant core of the cone. Fir

The taproot of a cottonwood must be in water. This conspicuous stand of cottonwoods demarcates the course of the Snake River, as well as many waterways in the West. Photo by Verne Huser.

cones rarely fall intact unless cut by squirrels or birds or blown down by strong winds. Spruce cones grow pendent and fall intact; they spread their seeds through squirrel storage or the disintegration of cones on the forest floor.

An old story, perhaps part myth, part–Native American lore, and part natural history, tells of the plight of the Douglas fir in ancient times. Mice found the seeds of the Douglas so delicious that the species almost died out for the paucity of young trees. The adult trees finally held a convention to determine how to deal with their reduced propagation rate. They decided to "clamp down" on the mice to prevent their eating the succulent seeds. And so it came to pass: if you examine a Douglas fir cone, all you will see is the dried tail and hind legs of the mice, which are actually the three-pronged bracts sticking out of the layered scales in each Douglas fir cone, a characteristic means of identification.

All pines have bunched needles except the single-leaf pinyon. All five members of the white pine family, which includes two that grow in Jackson Hole, have five needles: white-bark pines in the Tetons normally grow at elevations above sixty-five hundred feet, limber pines at elevations below seventy-five hundred. An overlap

Plant succession is often evident along the river. Low-growing willows colonize first, followed by deciduous cottonwood trees, which are succeeded by conifers such as the blue spruce pictured here. A bull moose placidly stands in the channel. Photo by Verne Huser.

A limber pine cone.
Photo by Verne Huser.

Lodgepole pines, short-lived and shallow-rooted, serve as nurse trees for climax species and then are sacrificed to plant succession.
Photo by Verne Huser.

occurs, but the five-needled pines along the river are almost certainly limber pines. Lodgepole pines, so named because Plains Indians used them for their tipi or lodge poles, normally have only two needles bound together at their base.

On the low river benches, aspens and lodgepole pines often colonize areas where the river has deposited enough silt to provide adequate soil and appropriate habitat. Aspen groves and lodgepole forests then serve as nurseries for climax forests of spruce, fir, and Douglas fir. Two juniper species also grow along the river: mountain common juniper, a low spreading shrub that grows along the river benches near Deadman's Bar; and Rocky Mountain juniper, a small tree that grows on the north wing of Blacktail Butte and a few places along the Snake, such as the riverbank just below 4 Lazy F Ranch a quarter mile above Menor's Ferry.

On low river benches, aspens often colonize and provide nurseries for climax forests of conifers. Photo by Verne Huser.

The Deadman's Bar Road, an unpaved spur off the Eastside Highway, provides access to the Snake River but also to a typical example of the plant succession pattern common to the valley. Lodgepole pine, a primary species that requires the heat of a fire to germinate, thrives there along with a few shrubby common junipers and an occasional young spruce or fir. Lodgepole pine, which grows well in open sunlight, provides the shade that enables the climax species of spruce and fir, which cannot tolerate open sunlight, to get their start. Short-lived and shallow-rooted, the pine serves as a nursery forest; once it has served its purpose, it dies, feeding the following climax forest with its dead debris. You will note numerous dead, down, and dying trees as the pattern tends toward climax and lodgepole pine is sacrificed to succession.

Mountain alder and several species of willows, plus silverberry (called wolf willow in Canada), buffaloberry, snowberry, serviceberry, chokecherry, red osier dogwood, huckleberry, and black hawthorn, along with common juniper, eventually fill in the understory. They help to hold soil and harbor silt when the river rises, and they provide valuable nutrients to their more robust plant neighbors. The understory also provides food for beavers and moose, which browse many of them heavily throughout the summer and well into the fall before snow covers them for the winter.

The tall, slender profiles of subalpine firs in the distance contrast sharply with the broader shape of the Douglas fir in the foreground.
Photo by Verne Huser.

Other flowering shrubs grow farther from the river. Antelope bitterbrush shows its tiny, pale-yellow, sweet-smelling flower blossoms in midsummer. Sagebrush, the pale-gray-green shrub that dominates so much of the valley floor, offers its inconspicuous whitish blossoms on tall stalks in late summer, and its spicy odor after a rain. The small bright-yellow waxy blooms of the shrubby cinquefoil appear in July. Wild roses grow in dense clumps and form bright-red vitamin C–rich hips in the late summer—I have seen porcupines feeding on them in the fall.

Careful observation coupled with a bit of knowledge enriches any experience on the river. As you float down the Snake River, look carefully at the shore. Which bank is the older? The question is not as strange as you may think, and understanding the processes of succession will make the answer to this question obvious. The vegetation along the river tells a story of constant change.

On the left bank you may see a forest of 120-year-old blue spruce trees, while the silt-covered bars on the right bank are covered with willows and young cottonwoods only a few inches high. The higher river bench a few feet inland is covered with ten-, fifteen-, twenty-foot-high cottonwoods, their bases marked by fingers of silt. Each tiny tree helps to slow down the current's velocity and, when it slows, allows the water to drop its suspended load of silt and sand.

Fingers of silt appear down-current from any obstacle that slows the flow, and grain upon grain of silt settles, replenishing the bank.

A silted bank covered with white seed-bearing cottonwood fluff is the nursery for the next generation of trees. In several places along the Snake you can see a series of annual riverbank tree nurseries: twenty feet from the current, tiny cottonwood trees grow in last year's silt, but fifty feet from the current, cottonwood trees four or five feet tall suggest earlier footing and rooting. A hundred feet from the current, trees fifteen to twenty feet tall thrive, and a few small spruce appear.

Floods contribute to plant succession patterns by undercutting the banks and causing trees to fall into the river. Carried downstream by a high, swift flood current, the trees lodge in shallow water and obstruct or slow the current. The trees almost always come to rest with their root systems upstream, their tops pointing the direction of the current. This is because the roots form the heaviest, bulkiest part of the tree and are the first feature of the trunk to catch bottom in shallower water. The top of the tree floats to a downstream position, leaving the roots to offer a massive surface obstacle to anything floating downstream, a snag that can obstruct debris or watercraft.

About two miles below Deadman's Bar on the left bank two spruce trees lean well out over the water. Undercut by floodwaters, they had started to fall. How long ago? The tops of the trees that grow straight up provide a clue: while the bases of the trees lean precipitously, the upward growth from the lean indicates the length of time the trees have been leaning. In 1959 I estimated that the two trees had been leaning for twelve to fifteen years, undercut somewhere between 1944 and 1947. It was not until 1996 that I learned 1943 had been a major flood year and that the two trees I had been observing for decades had in fact been undercut by a flood fifty-three years earlier.

During flood seasons the river rises almost to the bank on which the old leaning giants grow. Once I feared these two spruces might be swept away with so many other undercut trees that fall into the river daily. But their situation is not as perilous as I once thought. If the river rises another foot on the left bank, it will flood the right bank, relieving the pressure on the left. The river will overflow the young willows and cottonwoods growing on the lower-level right bank, and these venerable spruce trees will survive the flood, as they have for decades.

The river serves as a significant and conspicuous agent of

A single beaver pond such as this one plays a dramatic and beneficial role in ecosystems, often a pattern of initiating plant succession.
Photo by Verne Huser.

change, but so do the relatively inconspicuous beavers. Trees cut by beavers often block channels, sometimes alter the river's flow at critical points, and occasionally result in the river's opening new channels, especially where beavers have dug canals as they frequently do along the Snake. Where beavers build dams on the smaller channels or in backwater ponds, the impoundments eventually silt in and become marshes, then revert to meadows, and begin to grow another generation of trees. Thus, a dramatic plant succession pattern can be initiated by only a few beavers.

I encourage my passengers to listen to the river. At high water levels you can hear the riverbed rocks, largely round quartzite cobble, rolling along the river bottom, sounding like popcorn popping. At lower water levels you can hear the sizzling sound of sand and silt, suspended in the water, flowing against the boat bottom, which amplifies the sound. Flowing water moves material: from huge boulders to tiny grains of silt, from giant spruce and cottonwood trees to plant seeds and insect larvae.

All this may sound like a lesson in river geology, and it is, but it is also a lesson in plant succession patterns. The tumbling rocks and shifting silt scour the river bottom, removing underwater vegetation that becomes part of the organic debris carried by the river, nutrients that assist new growth in silt beds laid down as water levels drop and new islands form.

Whenever the current slows, it drops its suspended load of gravel, sand, and silt that form gravel islands, sandbars, and silt beds. These in turn catch more river-borne debris, enlarge and stabilize the islands, further slowing the current and sending it in other directions, effecting further cutting elsewhere.

As new islands form, they support more plant life, which stabilizes the islands; they continue to enlarge. Some may ultimately join the shore. Even if high waters overflow the bank, a new layer of silt may be added with nutrients that help plants grow bigger and faster, further stabilizing the bank—until a bigger flood washes it all away—trees, shrubs, flowers, and soil, and the whole process begins again.

Not long ago Frank Ewing told me of a recent float trip he had taken on the Pacific Creek–to–Moose segment of the Snake where he and I guided in 1959-1960 for the Grand Teton Lodge Company. He rarely travels that section of river, now that his business is running whitewater trips in the canyon, but he did in mid-June 1998. He was amazed at the differences he found: "I knew where I was with respect to major points along the river, but I was totally lost as to specific channels. I might have been on a completely new river; in fact, I was." You can imagine how stunned I was by the changes I noticed, coming back to the river in 1992 after twenty years of only casual visits to Jackson Hole.

To some extent, you can witness these same changes yourself even over the course of a single float trip. What you will be seeing, of course, is only a snapshot of the longer processes under way around you. But you will be able to read a great deal into that snapshot by observing and playing detective, asking questions and puzzling out answers through research in the field and in the library, by going to ranger talks and taking float trips with knowledgeable guides (many of whom augment the park service naturalist programs).

Wildflowers

In the early 1990s yellow-blooming sweet clover (sometimes called simply yellow clover) became the dominant vegetation along the Snake River shoreline and islands as well as along the park's highways. A nonnative invasive weed, it came into the valley with

Arrowleaf balsamroot. Photo by Verne Huser.

the livestock industry. Few animals, domestic or wild, will eat it because it grows tough and tastes bitter. Tiny sweet clover seeds lie hidden in the hay that ranchers feed their livestock; the seeds flow with the spring snowmelt, take root wherever they land, and produce a growth of tall, sweet-smelling clover in the spring.

Many of the seeds wind up in the Snake River, obliterating such native wildflowers as willow weed (known as river beauty in Alaska), pink monkey flowers, Indian paintbrush, even gentian. Before the floods of the mid-1990s the river islands turned yellow in midsummer with sweet clover to the detriment of native species and the natural diversity and floral color along the river. Two flood years, however, have scoured the islands clean of clover, and native forbs (broad-leaved flowering plants) have reestablished themselves in Snake River bottomlands.

The Snake offers floaters from mid-May through mid-October a wonderful display of the area's wildflowers. Earth dampened by snowmelt encourages early flowers: tiny yellow ranunculus (commonly called buttercups), pink-and-white spring beauties, rare subtle magenta shades of exotic steersheads, both purple and yellow violets, pale-purple ball-head waterleaf (also known as catsbreeches), and marsh marigolds of the palest yellow.

Yellow flowers seem to dominate spring. Pastures blaze with dandelions, while the drier slopes and sagebrush flats break out in

Mules-ears. Photo by
Verne Huser.

the huge bright-yellow blossoms of arrowleaf balsam root, which almost hide the deep purple of low larkspur and sugarbowl or Douglas clematis. The balsam root has pale-green basal leaves and blooms earlier than an equally conspicuous plant known as mules-ears. The two are often confused, but mules-ears have darker green leaves that alternate up the stem and generally bloom later than balsam root.

Early in the floating season, the wildflowers may be more obvious and spectacular above the Snake than on it, for the high water may inundate many species, and snowbanks often persist along some riverbanks until early July. Shuttle drives to and from the river and around the valley offer special opportunities to see a wide variety of flowers in the spring and to watch the continually evolving display throughout the summer and into fall.

As longer days and more direct sunlight warm the earth, new flowers appear daily—three, four, five, or more species each day. I have counted more than fifty species in a brief walk at both the Pacific Creek launch site and the Grand Teton Lodge Company's meal site at Deadman's Bar.

Morel mushrooms appear as damp ground warms. A special sub-species thrives the year following a fire, especially near aspen groves. During the spring of 1996, the year after a burn on Antelope Flats, I harvested a peck or more for frying and drying. They are delicious additions to any meal, but the usual caveat regarding mushrooming applies: you must know what you are picking.

On the unpaved road from the Eastside Highway to the Deadman's Bar launch site, you can see a few pine-filled potholes to the right (northwest) of the gravel road at the turnoff. After dropping down a steep incline (intermittently paved to prevent the formation of moguls) and passing through a mixed-conifer forest that grows on the edge of the moraine, you will see wildflowers blooming along the road, different species flowering in natural sequence throughout the season: wild geraniums, wild flax, columbine, oysterplant or salsify, phlox, and mountain bluebells.

Bluish purple lupine contrasts with scarlet gilia and yellow wooly aster in the sagebrush at the Deadman's Bar turnoff; a week later wild buckwheat comes out, pale green at first, then yellow, ripening to a rusty red. The purplish blue harebell, the white yarrow, and the showy fleabane daisy with its yellow-centered, purple-fringed blossom brighten the roadway. Wild geraniums bloom deep reddish purple, fading to pink, then to white as the summer sun begins to bear down on them.

Several clumps of creamy-white columbine bloom briefly along with heart-leafed arnica in the shade on the left (south) as you begin to descend the first hill. Other shade-loving species—twin flowers, a wide variety of orchids (fairyslipper or calypso and both spotted and striped coralroot), a purple-blooming vine clematis, pipsissewa, wild strawberries—decorate the left bank (south) of the road cut. To the right (north), western bedstraw appears along with wild roses, penstemon, paintbrush, and serviceberry as the road turns left (west) through the lodgepole pine forest. Common juniper crowds the road in places, and both goldenrod and purple asters bloom later in the summer along with tall magenta fireweed.

The road flattens out through a lodgepole pine forest on a broad river bench. A steep grade follows (also paved for a few dozen yards), dropping to a lower river terrace covered with sagebrush and bitterbrush, a major browse plant for members of the deer family, which includes elk, as well as bison. On this lower bench shooting stars, prairie smoke (also known as long-plumed avens), and larkspur have given way to wild buckwheat, groundsel, and stonecrop. Pink pusseytoes appear here later in the summer along

Prairie smoke.
Photo by Verne Huser.

with needlegrass or speargrass, a *stipa* that produces tiny, sharp arrowlike seeds with tails; you can throw them like small spears.

The only trees along this bench, aspens and lodgepole pines, grow in old river channels where deposits of ancient river silt make tree growth possible. Both trees represent primary species that set the stage for mature conifer forests in years to come. One more slight drop in the road brings you to the launch site; a road off to the left leads to the Lodge Company's meal site.

At the launch site a few broad-leafed cottonwoods contrast with the riverside narrow-leafed variety, and blue spruces line the river-bank. Across the river you can see a few limber pines near the river and halfway up the steep cut bank. Several species of wildflowers bloom here as the season progresses: wild roses, stonecrop, fire-weed, purple asters, pussytoes, arnica, and many more.

On the river itself you may find several water-loving species of wildflowers: the elephanthead, a stalk carrying dozens of tiny ele-phant-head-like blossoms composed of pink ears and purple trunks; grass of Parnassas, an exotic-looking five-petaled white flower; blue-eyed grass, lone yellow-centered flowers with five bluish purple petals on a grasslike stalk; and yellow monkey flow-ers named for the simian-faced pattern of their blossom.

Taller, more robust water lovers include the large white-umbelled cow parsnip; the western coneflower, a rayless sunflower

Pinedrops.
Photo by Verne Huser.

with only disc flowers; and monkshood, a deep-purple relative of the low larkspur. All of them may grow to a height of five or six feet. As Richard Shaw points out in his book on wildflowers of the region, *Plants of Yellowstone and Grand Teton National Parks*, monkshood, normally purple, also appear as albinos.

In drier areas other giants grow: elkweed or green gentian may reach four or five feet in height, its flowers, pale-green petals with purple spots, climbing the tall stalk. Wild hollyhocks up to three and four feet tall grow along the main Eastside Highway and at the Snake River Overlook. The pinedrop, a *mycrotroph* that lives on soil fungus, may also grow to a height of three or four feet as may the giant hyssop.

Several points along the Snake offer special wildflower attractions. At the mouth of Cottonwood Creek in the park (there are three Cottonwood Creeks that enter the Snake in its roughly hundred-mile course covered by this book), yellow monkey flowers bloom in abundance, then forget-me-nots paint a pale-blue line across this delta between water and alder. Rocky Mountain fringed gentian bloom on several midriver islands (Buffalo Channels, the Spread, Schwabacher Island, Teton Marsh), and blue penstemon bloom on the dry hillside on the right a mile below the Lodge Company's meal site. Chokecherries, baneberry, and serviceberry all bloom along the river, and in early summer the tiny, inconspicuous yellow blossoms of silverberry perfume the river with their exotic fragrance. Moose feed heavily upon its silver-gray foliage.

Flowers appear and disappear with the seasonal changes. Each summer I am pleasantly surprised to see new flowers blooming where I have never seen them before, and disappointed to see old friends gone—like the pink monkey flower (*Mimulus lewisia,* named for Meriwether Lewis on the Lewis and Clark Expedition) that once grew at the base of the right bank of the right-hand channel in the Maze and the river beauties that once grew on a gravel island near an abandoned eagle's nest, the result of flood scouring.

The vegetation feeds the wildlife. Flowering plants are known to the botanist as forbs; they provide much of the food for members of the deer family, for bison and bighorn sheep and many smaller grazers and browsers, all animals that may eat grass but augment their diet with forbs and other plants. Browsers such as moose feed on leaves, twigs, and buds. Beavers feed on the cambium, or growth layer, between the outer bark and the wood of many deciduous trees and shrubs. Insects also feed on these plants, providing food for birds, amphibians, and small mammals.

Hummingbirds not only feed on the nectar of flowering plants but also eat mosquitoes. Dragon flies too feed on insects and insect larvae that in turn feed on plant detritus. Many of the swallows nest in riverside or beaver-pond shrubs and feed on insects that hatch in the water after larval life, feeding on underwater plant and animal detritus. One reason park visitors are asked not to collect firewood in the park is that dead-and-down wood provides food and lodging for many insects that provide food for higher life-forms—higher in the food chain, not in any hierarchy of animal worth.

As wildlife biologist Adolph Murie told me many years ago, "If you want to understand wildlife, you've got to know the plants, because the entire pattern of life begins with them." Knowing something about wildflowers helps us appreciate them, and as you learn to identify them, your appreciation will grow. I recommend one of Richard Shaw's many books on the wildflowers of Jackson Hole or the *Field Guide to Rocky Mountain Wildflowers* that the Craighead brothers, Frank and John, helped put together. Frank's book *For Everything There Is a Season,* which traces the sequence of natural events in the Grand Teton–Yellowstone area, is an ideal guide to what blooms when and where.

In the early days of river floating, guides were permitted to land their passengers to explore the shoreline, and we thus saw many more wildflowers. Today, scenic floaters are not allowed to stop—though fishing guides still can and do, often setting up day camps complete with picnic tables and chairs for their clients who unfortunately are often oblivious to the riverside vegetation they are trampling and the wildlife they are disturbing. Noncommercial watercraft may still stop along the shoreline. If you do, enjoy the plants and the animals you see, but choose where you walk with respect and awareness.

The Muries

Olaus (1889–1963) and Adolph (1899-1974) Murie were half brothers of Norwegian ancestry who lived their latter lives in Jackson Hole. Early wildlife biologists, they spent many years doing pioneer wildlife research in Alaska, Canada, and elsewhere. Both Olaus and Ade worked for the old U.S. Biological Survey, forerunner of the U.S. Fish and Wildlife Service. They married half sisters whom they met in Alaska, Margaret (Mardy) and Louise (Weezy), and the couples eventually settled on a ranch along the Snake River at the foot of the Teton Range.

In 1927 Olaus and Mardy moved to Jackson Hole, where Olaus was assigned to study the elk, or wapiti, and ultimately produced *The Elk of North America* (1951), the definitive study of the species. Olaus and Mardy together wrote a book about their life in Jackson Hole, *Wapiti Wilderness* (1967). Mardy published *Journeys to the Far North* (1973) from Olaus's field notes a decade after his death, and compiled and edited *The Alaskan Bird Sketches of Olaus Murie* (1979).

Olaus, a fine self-taught artist and a keen observer of the natural world, illustrated his own books as well as those of his wife and his brother. He also illustrated J. Frank Dobie's *Voice of the Coyote*.

In an antipark lawsuit in the mid-1940s Olaus, serving as an expert witness, established the scientific importance of Jackson Hole. He served on the board of directors for the Jackson Hole Preserve, Inc., which managed the Rockefeller lands during the biggest feud over land use in the valley's history. Olaus fervently opposed Rockefeller's idea of opening a wildlife exhibit of penned animals in the park. In *Crucible for Conservation,* the most comprehensive analysis of the bitter battle over the establishment, then the enlargement, of Grand Teton National Park, Robert Righter characterizes Olaus as "a man who combined scientific knowledge and love of wilderness with honesty and openness."

Adolph's assignment to study coyotes in Yellowstone led to his *Ecology of the Coyote in the Yellowstone* (1940). Two books about the wolves and grizzly bears of Alaska, where Ade spent some thirty summers of his life, followed. *The Wolves of Mount McKinley* (1944) is considered a seminal work for all ecological studies that succeeded it.

From their Jackson Hole ranch, the Muries continued their work and their writing: Olaus wrote and illustrated *A Field Guide to Animal Tracks* (1954), one of the first books in the Houghton Mifflin Peterson Field Guide Series. Many of the Murie track casts, scats, and study skins used to produce that book now reside in the museum at the Teton Science School.

Olaus, who helped found the Wilderness Society in the mid-1930s and served as its president and director for many years, died in 1963. Mardy was devastated. Brock Evans, then a Pacific Northwest (now a Washington, D.C.) conservation leader, put Mardy to work in her natural arena, the environmental movement, where she thrived and developed her own leadership role. Numerous conservation awards recognized Mardy's contributions, and in 1998 she received a Presidential Medal. Her participation in public and congressional hearings, her writing, both sensitive and direct, and her inspiring talks about wilderness made her a leader in the field.[1]

Mardy also inspired the Teton Science School, which was founded by Ted Major in 1971, led fund-raising efforts for the school, and gave a large part of the Murie collection to the school (the remainder resides at the Smithsonian).

Adolph, the younger brother, died in 1974. Although I never met Olaus—he died before I moved to the Hole—I did get to know Ade and spent many hours with him during his latter years. I learned much from him, admired him greatly, and enjoyed developing a personal relationship with him and his wife, Louise, on the Murie Ranch on the Snake River just south of Moose. Holding his hand, I rode to the hospital in the ambulance with a semiconscious Ade when he had the first attack of the

1. Mardy is the subject of a documentary film being produced by Charlie Craighead and Bonnie Kreps, both of whom appear elsewhere in this section. Out of his respect for Mardy, Harrison Ford, who generally does not do such things, serves as narrator for the film, and John Denver's special song written for Mardy will be featured in the film, Arctic Dance: The Mardy Murie Story. The film features Terry Tempest Williams, a former Teton Science School student and teacher whom Mardy inspired and who now inspires Mardy.

Margaret "Mardy" Murie, along with her husband, Olaus, brother-in-law, Adolph and his wife, Louise, were pioneers of wildlife research and conservation in the Jackson Hole area and throughout the United States. Photo by Verne Huser.

malady that eventually led to his death. I still miss our conversations about wildlife and wilderness.

Ade did not believe in marking animals to study them; he believed, as Margaret Altmann did, that naturalists should learn to observe animals in their natural habitat, live with the animals, get to know them without disturbing them. He was in full support of returning wolves to the Yellowstone ecosystem and of letting natural wildfires burn.

Louise, a quiet but impressive environmentalist in her own right, now lives in Jackson, but Mardy remains on the Murie Ranch, which will someday become the Murie Center, an environmental and wildlife research facility, associated with the Teton Science School but with a different board, focus, and function. Its mission, according to the center's brochure, will be "to recreate the magic of a typical day on the Murie Ranch in the 1950s, to bring together a diversity of individuals, let them coalesce into small groups in the informal and inspiring atmosphere of the ranch, and stimulate them with significant issues involving the relationship between humans and wild nature."

PAUL M. HAUSER   FEB. 1999

Snake River Wildlife

The wildlife, as varied and abundant as on any floatable river south of the Canadian border, offers one of the most enjoyable elements of the Snake River, whether observed from the river or from the shore, on foot or on snowshoe, by bike or by car. The riverine environment attracts creatures that merely drink at the river as well as those that depend on it for essential habitat, for food and shelter, for nesting sites and building material, for cover and transportation, and for protection from their natural enemies.

Beavers are a good example of an animal whose lifeways are inextricably linked to the river. They cut trees near the water, where vegetation offers cover from mountain lions, eagles, or bears, and should predators be present, they slap their tails on the surface of the water as a warning to other beavers. Branches ferried through the water to beaver lodges or dens provide litter and building materials and food for the vegetarian beaver. The beaver must be in water to defecate and is reported to mate in the water.

Otters feed on fish, frogs, and crayfish that live in or near water. They swim for food and fun, traveling with the current or against it, diving into the river to escape predators and to catch trout. Osprey and bald eagles, kingfishers and white pelicans, great blue heron and American mergansers all feed on fish that live in the river. Heron, eagles, and osprey usually nest in tall trees that grow near the riverbank, kingfishers in the high cut banks along the river, and pelicans on islands in lakes fed by rivers (once in Jackson Hole, found now primarily in Yellowstone in this region).

Moose feed on water plants and may bear young on islands in the river, protected from predators by deep channels or swift water, effectively hidden in the willow and alder thickets that grow along the river.

With so many creatures dependent upon the river and its life-giving waters, is it any wonder that float trips on the Snake offer such excellent wildlife observation opportunities? People ask the guides, "What wildlife will we see?" as they drive to the launch site. It depends on the time of year, the time of day, the phase of the moon, even the behavior of the passengers, but there are no guarantees.

A great blue heron rookery in the winter-bare branches of cottonwood trees along the Snake River. Photo by Verne Huser.

The Snake River is a natural area, not a Disneyland theme park. The best bet is to be quiet, as unobtrusive as possible.

Occasionally, this point is lost on visitors. On a trip in the late 1950s one of my passengers could talk about nothing but moose: "When are we going to see a moose?" she asked constantly. "Is this good moose country? Where are all the moose I've been hearing about?" I finally spotted a big bull lying down in the alders, trying to beat the heat, the flies and mosquitoes. We could barely see his antlers, but I pointed him out for her, saying, "Here's your moose."

The woman was indignant. "Why doesn't he get up?" She stood up in the boat and yelled, "Hey, Mister Moose, get up and walk around." I told her to be quiet. How would she like a perfect stranger coming into her bedroom some morning and saying, "Hey, Mrs. Jones, on your feet!"?

We should all remember that we are guests in the home of dozens of species of wildlife and have no right to disturb their peace.

Reptiles and Amphibians

Only four species of reptiles have been reported in Jackson Hole, all of them snakes and all found along the Snake River: two species of garter snakes, the wandering and the common; the rubber boa, which I have seen near String Lake as well as at RKO Camp; and the bull snake (skin casts have been found, but few sightings have been made). Winters are too cold, the elevation too high for most reptiles. There are no turtles and only one rare lizard, the sagebrush.

Among the amphibians native to the valley of the Upper Snake are two frogs (the spotted and the boreal chorus), one toad (the boreal), and a single salamander species (the tiger). All are found along the river itself. The leopard frog existed in the watershed in the mid-1950s, but it seems to have disappeared since then, perhaps one of the losses in a modern worldwide pattern of amphibian extinction.

The Craigheads

Frank C. Jr. and John J. Craighead, twin wildlife biologists, are as much a part of the Snake River to me as the cottonwoods and blue spruces that grow on the riverbanks. I have seen them dozens of times, fly-fishing from shore, from their little Avon Redshank boat, or from a midriver gravel bar, braced against the current in their hip waders.

Born in 1916, the two moved to Jackson Hole in the mid-1940s, built log cabin homes, raised families, and conducted their research on numerous wildlife species: hawks and owls, bald eagles on the Snake River, grizzly bears in Yellowstone, and golden eagles in Montana. They pioneered radio telemetry, the practice of tracking certain species of wildlife with radio collars to follow their life patterns and better understand their behavior.

Seeing the animals they studied decimated by the abuse of rivers— dam building, dewatering, development, channelization, and pollution—they became interested in protecting natural rivers in other western states and in the East as well. They participated in drafting the National Wild and Scenic Rivers Act—in fact, the legislation was their idea.

The brothers wrote their first article for *National Geographic*, "Adventures with Birds of Prey," in 1937 when they were barely out of their teens. During and after World War II they continued to write for the

Frank (left) and John Craighead fish the fast water of the Snake River below Jackson Lake dam. Photo by Shirley Craighead.

magazine with a dozen articles appearing between 1940 and 1976 on subjects as varied as falconry and survival skills, grizzly bears and white-water rafting.

With Ray J. Davis, they coauthored *Rocky Mountain Wildflowers* in the Peterson Field Guide Series. Frank wrote *Track of the Grizzly* (1982) about the twins' decade-long research on grizzly bears in Yellowstone and *For Everything There Is a Season* (1994), which outlines when to expect what wildflowers to bloom and what wildlife to appear or breed or nest in both Grand Teton and Yellowstone National Parks. Their sister, Jean Craighead George, has written numerous books on natural history subjects for children and young adults, including the ever popular, New-berry Award–winning *Julie of the Wolves*.

Like their parents, the Craighead children have a special affinity for the natural world: Karen, Derek, and John are John's children; Lance, Charlie, and Jana are Frank's. Karen and Derek wrote a *National Geographic* article about a backpacking trip through Yellowstone in 1972, the park's centennial year, and Karen has since published a book on the wildlife of Jackson Hole. Charlie has photographed for that magazine and published several books, including *"Who Ate the Backyard?": Living with Wildlife on Private Land* (1997). He was the coproducer, director of cinematography, and cowriter (with Bonnie Kreps) for a documentary film about Mardy Murie, *Arctic Dance*.

When the Craighead children were teenagers, they frequently participated in their fathers' research. Jana, a student of mine when I taught high school English in Jackson, raised a pet kestrel she once brought to class. Lance has followed directly in his father's and uncle's footsteps with his study of bears in Alaska.

While running the Salmon River rapids, Charlie and Derek were wired to check their pulses, respiration rates, body temperatures, and various other physical and physiological reactions to the adrenaline rush of running whitewater. Charlie and Derek provided photographs for one of their fathers' *National Geographic* articles in 1967 when the boys were still in high school. They also ran frequent float trips on the Snake, one summer advertising a phantom river trip company called Stark Terror Float Trips.

The elder Craigheads remain as much a part of the Jackson Hole and the Snake River as the wildlife they have studied there for more than a half century, as much a part of the Snake River as the gravel bars and riffles where they fish.

Fish

Native cutthroat trout, so named because of the reddish slash near their gills, have been decimated by the introduction into the Snake River watershed of exotic species that both hybridize and compete with them. The cutthroat trout is the only endemic trout in the Snake River drainage. Its range is considerably smaller than the historic range of the Yellowstone cutthroat, restricted to the Snake above Palisades Dam and the Gros Ventre River. The U.S. Fish Commission introduced German browns and lake trout into the Snake River watershed in 1890; the Wyoming Game and Fish Department introduced both brook and rainbow trout to the area in 1933. In 1973 I spent ten days in southern Yellowstone's Snake River drainage. Our party caught plenty of fish—German browns, rainbows, eastern brookies, lake trout—but not a single native cutthroat. Only native cutthroat trout are currently being planted in the Snake, but remnant populations and hybrids of all the exotic species remain.

Another planting of exotic species has occurred in Kelly Warm Springs a mile north of Kelly on the road up the Gros Ventre River: tropical fish that valley residents have eliminated from their home aquariums and dumped into the warm waters of this natural spring-fed pond where they have propagated. Great blue heron and kingfishers frequently congregate to feed on the colorful array of menu choices, while local human residents visit to restock their aquariums from the new generations of exotic fish.

Mackinaw trout have been introduced into Jackson Lake and get into the river, both above the lake and below the dam. Today lake trout exist in many lakes of the Upper Snake River drainage, but browns seem to find only Jackson Lake and the Snake River as suitable habitats. In recent years a serious problem of predation on native species by lake trout in Yellowstone Lake has given fishery biologists concern. There is also fear that whirling disease found in trout species in the adjacent states of Idaho and Montana might migrate into Jackson Hole, but to date there is no evidence of spreading infection.

Mountain whitefish abound in the Snake River; local fishermen used to snag them from the bridge across the Snake (an illegal practice now) at Flagg Ranch for winter food supply, smoking and drying the bony fish. At certain times whitefish will take dry flies, especially flies decorated with bright red. Three species of suckers feed along the Snake River bottom: both speckled and long-nosed dace and Bonneville redside shiners, along with two species of chub and two of sculpin. It is no wonder so many fish-eating birds thrive along the Snake.

Fishing the Snake River has become a major recreational activity in recent years. Snake River fishermen once used boats primarily to reach good fishing holes, but now they float fish and stop to bank fish.

Birds

Large, spectacular birds such as the white pelican, bald eagle, osprey, great blue heron, sandhill crane, and Canada goose frequent the Snake River riparian zone. On a few rare occasions in recent decades, trumpeter swans, which nest nearby, have made their appearance along the river. On the initial Grand Teton Lodge Company float trip in early June 1960 a pair of trumpeters saluted the raft I was guiding as we launched, trumpeting as they flew past—the thrill of a lifetime for me and my passengers.

The Grand Teton National Park bird checklist includes three hundred species, not all of which will be found along the Snake River, but a good many of them are, including many summer visitors and nesting residents. Rivers offer excellent birding opportunities, and

A quartet of trumpeter swans takes flight. Courtesy of Dick Barker.

many park visitors rack up "lifers" (birds seen for the first time in their lives) on the Snake River. Students at the National Audubon Society's Audubon Camp of the West near Dubois, Wyoming (just over Towgotee Pass from Jackson Hole), take a Snake River float trip as part of their regular program, and students at the Teton Science School frequently float the Snake, looking for birds.

Passengers often ask, "What's that black-and-white bird with the long tail?" The magpie is a novelty for most of my passengers from the East where this species does not exist. And when they ask, "What's the black bird with the yellow head?" or "What's that black bird with the red wing patch?" and I tell them that they have seen a yellowheaded or a red-winged blackbird, they think I am pulling their leg. A few observant folks have been lucky enough to see a yellow-and-black bird with a red head: the western tanager, a forest dweller we sometimes see on the river. Yellow warblers are also common along the Snake.

The most common duck on the Snake is the fish-eating American or common merganser. Males look stunning in their black-and-white spring breeding plumage (actually the "black" head is such a dark iridescent green that it appears black), but they molt in early summer and afterward look much like the females, a dull gray and

Yellow-headed blackbirds. Photo by Verne Huser.

rusty brown. Mergansers have "baby-sitting pools": you may see a hen with fifteen or twenty ducklings, then around the bend find a trio of hens sunning themselves on a gravel bar. Mergansers are delightful to watch, propelling themselves across the water like little motorboats, and difficult to count when they are bobbing underwater after fish.

Mallards and teal—green-winged, cinnamon, blue-winged—like the quiet water of shallow sloughs, beaver ponds, and backwaters, but we often see them in flight along the river, occasionally at the edge of the flow in the slower side channels. When they fly, it is easy to differentiate the smaller, faster teal—models built for speed in the duck world—from the mallards. Both Barrow's and common goldeneyes nest along the river, and we often see them in late June or early July with broods of ducklings, especially in confluence eddies where two channels meet.

We find few other ducks on the river, but several species seasonally frequent ponds in the watershed near the river as they pass through Jackson Hole: northern shovelers, ruddy ducks, gadwall, American wigeon, northern pintails, redheads, and ringnecked. Harlequin ducks are found wherever the water is cold, clear, and swift as it tends to be in Flagg Canyon and in many headwater streams in southern Yellowstone.

Special treats include avocets, which we see two or three times a summer; black terns, which I have seen only a half-dozen times in forty years on the river; Wilson's snipe, which nests in marshy areas; and Franklin gulls, which appear every season for a day or two when there is an especially big hatch of stoneflies.

The most common bird along the shoreline and the smallest is the spotted sandpiper. As it flies low over the water, it looks as though it has four wings because it flutters them so rapidly. After it lands, the sandpiper bobs its tail up and down, suggesting its common name, teeter-tail. The dipper or water ouzel is another bobber: it does deep knee bends when it lands on midstream rocks, then dives into the torrent after aquatic invertebrates. One hundred seventy aquatic invertebrate species appear on the park checklist, including caddisflies, stoneflies, and true flies. Dippers have nested at several places along the Snake, but they thrive in the fast-flowing mountain streams.

Five species of swallows live along the river: the barn, the only one with a true forked swallow tail and with an orange or buffy breast; the cliff, which builds its nest of mud under bridges and has a distinctive pattern on its forehead; the violet-green, which often appears just before a storm and flashes iridescent as sunlight catches its feathers; the tree, which has a darker bluish back and flashes iridescent purple; and the bank, which burrows into the riverbank and nests at the end of a tunnel several inches long. Bank swallows occur most frequently on the river except near bridges where cliff swallows dominate.

Several raptors appear along the river. Red-tailed hawks vie with osprey for nest sites, while osprey battle bald eagles for fish. Northern harriers sweep low, hunting over riverside wetlands. Northern goshawks hunt grouse, and kestrels feed on the late-summer grasshoppers that feed on ripening vegetation. Swainson's hawks hunt along the shoreline. Cooper's and sharp-shinned hawks keep the passerines (perching birds) alert. Peregrine falcons have been reported in recent years, more frequently in the mountains, but they must surely find good hunting along the Snake, where so many ducks make their homes.

Eagles, both golden and bald, do not migrate but remain in Jackson Hole. The golden eagle hunts in the grasslands and nests in the mountains, but the bald eagle dominates the Snake River, where it has nested successfully for at least as long as float trips have been running the Snake.

One pair of eagles raised young in the same nest in a large dead cottonwood on a shallow loop of the Snake about three miles below Deadman's Bar nearly every year from 1956 until 1973. That year

A bald eagle watches intently for fish in the Snake River. Photo by
Verne Huser.

the nest tree blew down in a severe windstorm, and all three eaglets,
only a week or two from fledging, died in the fall. The pair built a
new nest the following year and successfully raised a lone eaglet.

Bald eagles live for as long as a half century and mate for life, but
if one adult dies, the other may mate again. Eagles normally lay
eggs in early March. The eggs hatch about mid-April, and the eaglets fledge in early July when they are roughly twelve weeks old.
The eaglets have almost always fledged between July 5 and 13. According to our year-to-year observations of the pair below Deadman's Bar, when the adults raised a single eaglet, it usually fledged
late; when they raised three, at least one always fledged early, probably pushed out of the too crowded nest by its siblings. Guide Al
Klagge reports seeing a fledging as early as June 30 from a three-
eaglet nest, as late as July 23 for a lone eaglet: the parent birds simply could not seem to coax the youngster away from the security of
the nest.

Nest trees can be felled by beavers, undercut by the river, blown
down by storms, and abandoned by the adults, but despite these vi-
cissitudes, and thanks to regulations protecting the eagles, the birds'
population is slowly recovering. Only two nesting pairs lived on the
segment of Snake River between the dam and Moose in the late
1950s. A recent report suggests that in 1994 six known bald eagle
nests existed along the river corridor in the park. Since the ban on
the use of DDT in 1972, bald eagles have increased their numbers
both in the park and nationwide.

Not so the osprey, which migrate to Mexico in the winter. With the river open all year, fishing is better in winter because the water is lower and usually quite clear (it turns muddy with the spring runoff). DDT is still used in Mexico where osprey winter and often absorb dangerously high doses, lethal in the sense that the osprey fail to produce young because their eggshells are too thin to survive nesting activity. While eagles may have very nearly a 100 percent reproduction rate on the Snake, osprey have as low as a 30 percent rate some seasons.

Owls thrive along the Snake, but because they usually hunt at night, they may not be seen on the river as often as other raptors. Occasionally, great horned and great gray owls will appear during the day. I have seen great grays in the daytime on the Colter Bay–Jackson Lake Lodge road, on the Moose-Wilson Road, and at the Murie Ranch but only once from the river. I know they live in the heavy timber along the Snake, though, and have heard them at night on a moonlight float trip.

The summer of 1961 four owlets and at least one adult appeared nearly every day for almost a month at the mouth of Spread Creek, and for several summers in the 1990s a pair of great horned owls nested in a hollow cottonwood tree near Menor's Ferry—we saw them nearly every evening and often during daylight hours as well. In the early days when we were allowed to stop and explore the river marge, we found a great horned owl nesting in a dead hollow tree in the middle of a beaver pond and for weeks were able to show our guests the adults and owlets during the fledging process.

Certainly, owls can be heard at night: the deep, soft, rhythmic, multinoted whooing of the great horned; the even deeper, repeated, hollow "HOOT" of the great gray; the eerie, bloodcurdling cry of the somewhat rare western screech; and the raspy, sawlike tone of the tiny saw-whet owl along the Snake. During winter months, the snowy owl from the Arctic may appear; both great horned and great gray winter along the Snake.

We hear sandhill cranes more often than we see them. They nest on the National Elk Refuge, in the Willow Flats below Jackson Lake Lodge, and along the river in several areas, but are generally out of sight of the float trips. The summer of 1996 a pair nested on an island just below the Lost Nest Channel within easy sight of passing boats, but the flood levels of early July drowned out the nest as high water first inundated the island, then washed it completely away. Whooping cranes have recently been released in Yellowstone; it is hoped they may begin showing up along the Snake.

A lone white pelican on
the wing above the Snake
River. Photo by
Verne Huser.

White pelicans were common on the river in the late 1950s and
early 1960s, then they disappeared for a couple of decades, perhaps
due to DDT poisoning before Congress outlawed its use. They are
back now, most often seen soaring high above the river but occasionally in great flocks on midriver gravel bars or at the Oxbow. In
the spring mating season males grow huge protuberances on their
bills, and pelican couples nest on islands in Yellowstone Lake during the summer.

Canada geese, which hold the reputation of nuisance birds in
many places, give the Snake River a lively atmosphere. They honk
and flap about during the adults' molting season, which occurs at
the very time the goslings are still featherless and flightless—
nature's way to ensure the adults stay with their vulnerable, fluffy,
yellow offspring. The upstream reservoir causes artificial delays in
nesting during the spring runoff. The geese nest when the water
seems to have reached its highest level; then, a few days before the
eggs are due to hatch, the reservoir fills, and excess snowmelt water
is dumped into the river, raising its level to flood stage and drown-
ing out the nests, destroying the nearly hatched eggs. Some years
only a tenth of the geese nest successfully; other years, nearly all
make it and the river is crowded with geese.

Kingfishers are common, nesting in holes they dig into the higher
cut banks along the Snake. Great blue heron have nested in colonies
(called rookeries) along the Snake in past years at the Oxbow and
on the Big Island at the Maze along a channel across from the mouth
of Cottonwood Creek, but though individual birds still appear

A pair of Canada geese with their week-old goslings know the Snake River better than most boatmen. Courtesy of Dick Barker.

frequently, no nesting activity seems to be going on at present. Rookeries are established, then are phased out naturally.

I have not seen them for years and even when I did they were not along the river, but long-billed curlews have nested on the National Elk Refuge. A pair attacked me in the spring of 1961 as they defended their nest area against my intrusion. That portion of the Elk Refuge has been declared off-limits to visitors for years. We see a number of shorebirds and upland game birds on the river from time to time, but few are among the regulars with the exception of killdeer, which are common but not numerous.

Four woodpeckers call the Snake River bottomlands home: the northern three-toed, the northern flicker, the downy, and the hairy. The latter two are similar in coloration but different in size, the downy being the smaller. Both northern and loggerhead shrikes occur occasionally along the Snake, and I have seen both Bohemian and cedar waxwings from the river.

Numerous smaller birds—several warblers (yellow, yellow-rumped, Townsend's, and Wilson's), Clark's nutcracker, pine siskins, both black-capped and mountain chickadees, kinglets, both house and marsh wrens, American goldfinch, various flycatchers, the western wood pewee, juncos, and sparrows—fill the riverside woods with song. Calliope hummingbirds visit during the warmer

Clark's nutcracker.
Photo by Verne Huser.

months. Such colorful species as western and mountain bluebirds, pine and evening grosbeaks, and, rarely, the Bullock's oriole and lazuli buntings add their vocalizations and bright colors.

The most common forest bird along the river, the robin, nests early and often. The black-headed grosbeak is fairly common along the river and, like the robin, is known for its melodic song. Townsend's solitaire, more rare and reclusive, pipes a fine song as well. The raucous cry of the gray jay, also known as the whiskey jack, the Canada jay, and the camp robber, rivals that of the dark-blue, black-crested Stellar's jay, also sometimes called camp robber for its audacious thefts from picnic tables.

Crows generally occur in cultivated areas, while ravens prefer the wilderness, but both live along the Snake. Crows tend to flock more than ravens, which often appear in family groups during summer months. The smaller crows flap their wings more frequently than ravens, which glide and soar, performing acrobatic barrel rolls and loops, cavorting over the river and above the peaks in the high country. Ravens' wedge-shaped tails help them fly more acrobatically than crows. The larger, heavier ravens remain sacred to many Native American tribes.

A bird we often observed flying high over the river—especially as we drifted through the Burned Ridge moraine or past the 4 Lazy F Ranch—is the Clark's nutcracker. A large gray bird with black wings and flashes of white on wing and tail, the nutcracker feeds on seeds found in the cones of limber and white-bark pines. Seen against the clear sky, the sun highlighting its white patches, the nutcracker is a handsome bird. But you are likely to hear it before you see it: its raucous cry is startling in its harshness. Sometimes called

A young Calliope hummingbird on the edge of a nest. One chick has already flown. Courtesy of Des Bartlett.

Clark's crow because it is a relative of the crow, the nutcracker was named for William Clark of the Lewis and Clark Expedition. (Lewis had a woodpecker named after him, a bird common on the Salmon River in Idaho, a Snake tributary, and in Hells Canyon of the Snake between Idaho and Oregon, but it is a rare visitor to Jackson Hole.)

At dusk the common nighthawk appears with swept-back white-barred wings, feeding on insects, climbing gradually in the fading light, topping out high above the river, and swooping down in a steep dive. When it spreads its wings to break the fall, it creates a loud roaring sound, the reason behind the common name bullbat: it flits about much like a bat and roars like a bull.

Well-known naturalist and author Terry Tempest Williams is an excellent birder who floated with me on an evening trip in 1996. Together we spotted a rare Townsend's solitaire, a deep-woods nesting bird; a flight of colorful cedar waxwings, hawking for insects; a family of mountain bluebirds playing flycatcher; even a nuthatch—all birds that the general public would likely have missed. Observant, knowledgeable, interested passengers who respect the natural world enhance any trip.

Birding can be excellent on the Snake and its adjacent wetlands if you know your birds and behave respectfully on the river. Cornell University ornithologist Olin S. Pettingill, who for many years wrote a bird-finding column for *Audubon Magazine,* turned the column over to me for the September–October 1968 issue. I listed forty-seven species seen on a ten-mile two-hour float trip on the Snake and fifty-six species on an all-day twenty-mile trip. Both figures represent typical sightings.

Bison search for forage in winter. Photo by Verne Huser.

Mammals

Jackson Hole is well known for its large mammals: bison, moose, mule deer, pronghorn, and especially elk. Bison and pronghorn are better known by their commonly used but misleading names. Unrelated to the antelope of East Africa, what we call antelope is more closely akin to the goat and is the only member of its species, more accurately called pronghorn. The only true buffalo, the cape buffalo of Africa and the water buffalo of Asia, do not exist naturally in America; what we call buffalo is technically a bison.

Perhaps to avoid any confusion the National Park Service uses the popular misnomer in a handout distributed throughout Yellowstone and Grand Teton National Parks: "MANY VISITORS HAVE BEEN GORED BY BUFFALO: Buffalo can weigh 2000 pounds and can sprint at 30 mph, three times faster than you can run. These animals may appear tame but are wild, unpredictable, and dangerous. DO NOT APPROACH BUFFALO."

In spring 1998 I found part of the Jackson Hole herd grazing near Kelly Warm Springs; they had broken down several fences and ruled the range. The summer of 1997 I watched part of the herd, several dozen animals, grazing across the Antelope Flats Road near the Teton Science School. They paid little attention to cars that traveled the road. I stayed in my pickup truck, but several tourists made foolish advances toward the huge beasts to get better pictures. Nearly every summer tourists in Yellowstone are injured by bison; two have been killed. It will happen in Grand Teton National Park sooner or later if people fail to heed park service warnings and common sense.

Although a native, the pronghorn was absent for decades from Jackson Hole, having been hunted out and decimated by harsh winters and heavy snows when its natural migration routes to the Red Desert were cut off by human activity and development. In the early 1970s small groups of pronghorn began to migrate into the valley. Many of the early migrants winter-killed, but the species persisted, some individuals migrating out in the fall to return in the spring, and others weathering the harsh winters in protected areas.

Pronghorn have become more prevalent along the Snake in recent decades, often crossing the river as boats drift by. As frail as they seem, they are strong swimmers. They feed on forbs, sedges, and grasses along the river bottom and on the sagebrush flats, migrating back and forth across the valley and up the Gros Ventre River.

The National Park Service once kept a small herd of bison captive in fenced areas near the Oxbow Bend of the Snake a few miles north of Jackson Lake Dam, part of the Jackson Hole Wildlife Exhibit, a pet project suggested by John D. Rockefeller Jr. When the whole herd escaped, a group of enterprising local cowboys was sent on a roundup but failed to accomplish a recapture. Instead, wildlife ethologist Margaret Altmann and her student assistant successfully drove the herd back by slowly making their presence known, showing themselves, snapping twigs, and letting their human odor drift into the herd. The third time the herd escaped, the wildlife authorities decided to let them have their freedom. Bison have been ranging freely throughout the valley for several decades since and have increased their numbers substantially. At one time there were as few as nine animals. Now there are more than three hundred.

During my first summer in Jackson Hole, when the herd numbered about eighteen animals, Margaret alerted me to the fact that the herd patriarch, a magnificent animal, was about to be deposed by two younger bulls. He was old, had grown a bit arthritic, and walked with a decided limp, but he was still an impressive beast with massive horns. As the fall rut began, we watched the

A bull elk stripping a lodgepole pine. Photo by Verne Huser.

preliminary battles, saw the clouds of dust raised by the bulls' paw-ing the earth, heard their rutting roars.

Not long afterward the old bull was dead; the two younger bulls continued the battle until one of them beat the other for the right to breed the cows. Saddened by the death of the old patriarch, Mar-garet suggested that had the animals not been confined, the old bull might have lived—he would have simply drifted away from the herd to live out his life alone. I remember her prediction now that the herd has free range of the valley and we often see older bulls alone.

Bison began appearing on the Snake in the late 1960s, shortly after they were allowed to range freely throughout the valley. I recall how excited we guides were when we first saw them. Now they appear once or twice every month, migrating to find favorite fodder.

Elk dominate the wildlife scene in Jackson Hole. Although most of the several thousand wapiti, as they were known by the Lakota, migrate to higher elevations for the summer, several hundred live along the Snake throughout the year, perhaps migrating a few miles south to the National Elk Refuge to escape the worst of the winter weather. Most of the elk that winter on the refuge cross the Snake during their spring and fall migration; their paths can be seen throughout the summer by close observers all along the benches that border the Snake. In late spring, many elk cows have their calves in the sheltered Snake River bottom, especially in the area around Pacific Creek. Small herds summer along the river, while others drop down to the river to drink at dusk and feed in the river bottom throughout the night. One herd spends the summer on the large marshy island known as the Big Island between Schwabacher Landing and the Bar B C Ranch.

By the mid-1970s the pressure from humans on the river forced the elk along the Snake to become nocturnal. They stayed off the river entirely while the boats were present, feeding and watering along the Snake overnight, from dusk to dawn, returning to cover in the early daylight hours. Nowadays you can see them inland at the dark edge of dusk, trickling across the sagebrush flats from the heavy timber of the Burned Ridge moraine, the potholes, and Timber Island. And if you rise early enough, you can see them reversing the pattern to return at dawn to the heavily timbered areas of the valley.

Although most elk summer in the higher elevations above Jackson Hole and in the Snake's Yellowstone headwaters, small herds remain on the valley floor. They often appear along the Snake River, especially at dawn and dusk.

Moose apparently came into the Jackson Hole area only about a century ago. Members of the Doane Expedition, traveling through Jackson Hole by river the winter of 1876-1877, reported only three moose—identifying them by sound, not by sight.

Some residents believe that the building of Jackson Lake Dam in the second decade of the twentieth century increased the moose population by providing them with more marsh area—willow flats watered by the raised water table. Whatever the reason, moose have become well established in Jackson Hole and can be seen on the river at any time of year at any time of day, though the late-afternoon trips usually produce the best sightings. Moose populations are declining, however, as park research biologist Douglas Houston, working in the early 1970s, predicted they would.

In the fall moose move out onto the sagebrush flats to feed on antelope bitterbrush until snow covers the low-lying shrub; in spring, as soon as the snow melts, the moose return to browse bitterbrush again after a winter of eating riparian willow twigs and bark. Moose browse (eat twigs and leaves) more than they graze on grass. Occasionally, you may see a moose on its knees, feeding on grasses or

A bull moose, its antlers in velvet, watches a boat drift by—well before the rutting season. Courtesy of Dick Barker.

sedges; the animals have such long legs and high shoulders that they have difficulty grazing grass. Their preferred food consists of buds and bark, leaves and flowering plants, and aquatic vegetation. The name *moose*, an Algonquian Indian word, means "twig eater." Because of its long legs and capacity to survive on twigs, the moose is better equipped to survive the deep snow and harsh Jackson Hole winters than most other members of the deer family.

Mule deer congregate during winter, often yarding up to share the responsibility of packing down the snow in good feeding areas. They frequent south-facing slopes such as the southern aspects of the Gros Ventre Buttes and Blacktail Butte, where direct sunlight melts the snow, giving the deer access to vegetation. Heavy snows force the deer down to river level and to low-elevation areas where they can find food. During summer months deer range more widely but in smaller groups, two or three or four, or often alone. Doe and their offspring make a common group; bucks sometimes travel in small groups until the fall rutting season. On the river we see deer frequently, though not as regularly as we see moose.

White-tailed deer were unheard of in Jackson Hole a few decades ago; I have not seen them on the river, but they have been reported in the area. Much more common in the eastern states, they seem to be extending their range to include the valley of the Upper Snake.

Bighorn sheep do not find the rugged slopes of the Tetons precarious. Photo by Verne Huser.

So is the raccoon. I had never seen one until the summer of 1996, when they began showing up on the left bank across the Snake from the 4 Lazy F Ranch—near the mouth of Ditch Creek. I suspect that someone had brought a few pet raccoons into the valley and they had either been released or escaped, but Al Klagge reports seeing raccoons at his home near Hoback Junction since the mid-1980s and having seen them on the river north of Moose for at least a decade.

Bighorn sheep live in the Gros Ventre Range and in the southern and western aspects of the Teton Range. They migrate seasonally across the Snake River, coming down the Gros Ventre drainage, then heading into the Tetons toward Buck Mountain and Mount Hunt. I once saw a trio on Blacktail Butte less than a half mile from the river. Bighorns live along the Gros Ventre and Hoback Rivers, both tributaries of the Snake, and in the sedimentary portions of the Tetons— I have seen them on the ridge that separates Darby Canyon into its two main forks. The bighorn populations are currently being threatened by disease spread by domestic sheep and by the loss and fragmentation of their habitat.

Bears abound in Jackson Hole, occurring all over the valley from mountaintop to river, but we see them rarely—only two or three times a summer, some summers not at all. Until recently, we thought only black bears were present in the Jackson Hole area and

A rare glimpse of a black bear. This one lingers near an elk carcass. Courtesy of Dick Barker.

that reports of grizzlies that lived in Yellowstone and the Teton Wilderness were only black bears, which can have fur that is black, brown, or cinnamon. However, the past decade has brought an increasing number of grizzly sightings, and grizzly attacks have occurred near Jackson Lake Lodge and in South Park as well as in the nearby Teton Wilderness. I have never seen a grizzly on the river, but I did see a youngster near Jackson Lake Junction the spring of 1996. It was livetrapped and relocated into the wilderness to protect both the bear and the tourists.

My most memorable bear sighting on the Snake occurred on my last trip of the 1993 season. Because other guides had been seeing bear, I suggested to my passengers that they keep their eyes peeled for bear. We had gone a mile or so downriver when one of my passengers pointed toward the bank. I turned to look, thinking, "This guy probably sees a beaver and doesn't know the difference," for we were in a good beaver area. But it was, in fact, a bear, a cinnamon-and-black cub, marked in a pattern I had not seen before. It reminded me of a young grizzly. The cub walked nonchalantly into the shallow water toward the boat.

A moment later a second similarly marked cub appeared, then it too entered the river, and the two began wrestling, boxing, playing in the water. We were not more than a hundred feet away when I saw the sow emerge from behind a bush, obviously a black bear.

She did not seem concerned about our presence. She and the yearling cubs, who were old enough to recognize danger, simply ignored us as we drifted past, only a few dozen yards away. I had never been closer to bears in the wild nor seen a more delightful display of their behavior.

Coyotes are common in Jackson Hole. Franz Camenzind studied them on the National Elk Refuge in the early 1970s; Olaus Murie had studied them in Jackson Hole a few decades before that; and Olaus's brother, Ade, had studied them in Yellowstone. Coyotes seem to fill the niche left when wolves disappear; in fact, one of the major battles that involves transplanted wolves in Yellowstone is against coyotes—and the wolves usually win. During the past few years wolves have been reported on the National Elk Refuge, on Teton Pass, and on the Salt River in Star Valley seventy miles south of Jackson. There is little doubt: the wolves have returned to their natural ecosystem in the valley of the Upper Snake.

Beavers appear every evening along the Snake River, feeding on willows, cottonwoods, and alders—almost any deciduous vegetation they can find near the water, which offers them protection from their enemies: coyotes, wolves, bears, cougars, even eagles and otters, which might attack young beavers. Along the river beavers find abundant food and ideal habitat.

In a sense two kinds of beavers inhabit the wetlands created by the Snake River: pond beavers and bank beavers. They are members of the same species but practice different lifestyles: bank beavers live in dens dug into the bank or in lodges built on the shore, often beneath the roots of a tree. Pond beavers build dams to create ponds or find some natural impoundment that offers the safety of a pond—water deep enough not to freeze solid in the winter.

During my 1973 trip on horseback through the headwaters of the Snake in the backcountry of southern Yellowstone, I found a half-acre area in which dozens of lodgepole pines had been cut, obviously by beavers, five or six feet above the ground. When I came upon an old beaver lodge with its top cut out, what had happened became apparent: beavers had built a lodge in a shallow pond, had been trapped in the lodge when the pond froze solid, and had cut their way out to live on lodgepole for the rest of the winter, cutting the trees from the top of the snowpack.

Because the Snake River rarely freezes, bank beavers can feed along its banks throughout the coldest weather, unlike the beavers living in lodges at the Oxbow where the quiet waters do freeze. Beavers are entirely vegetarian and do not migrate to lower, warmer

A beaver in his favorite element. Courtesy of Dick Barker.

elevations or hibernate; consequently, they must have food available year-round. If they live in a pond, they need to store enough bark and branches underwater to see them through the winter months, which in Jackson Hole may be as long as six months. During summer months beavers tend to be nocturnal because it is simply too hot to work in a fur coat during the heat of the day.

Through the construction of its lodges and the impounding of water, the beaver alters its habitat more than any nonhuman creature. Pond beavers usually build their lodges in the middle of the impoundment, but occasionally they will build on the bank. As long as their lodge has an underwater entrance to keep intruders out and a solid core of stout sticks to prevent other predators from digging them out, they are safe. A beaver cannot build a domed structure, but it can build a domed pile of sticks, then hollow out living quarters from within. The lodge breathes, air flowing both in and out through the spaces between its sticks and branches. In fact, during cold weather you can see steam from beavers' respiration rising from the lodge.

Beaver scent piles line the river, but you rarely see them unless you know what to look for: a pile of mud and debris with an oily, strong-smelling substance darkening it. Although the scent pile may look revolting, it has a fragrant odor from castoreum, a secretion of the beaver's castoreum glands near its tail that is used both

A marmot tentatively crosses a trail. Photo by Verne Huser.

in trapping beaver and in making perfume. As the first cool breeze of evening wafts across the water, the odor of castor tells you that beavers are about.

Beavers eat buds and leaves and the inner bark of most deciduous trees. Known as cambium, this cell-producing layer between bark and wood is broken down in the beaver's digestive system by special enzymes. It provides the most important food for Jackson Hole beavers, though in some areas they are known to feed on alfalfa or field corn—any kind of nutritious vegetation. However, beavers need to chew on hard material to keep their teeth honed for cutting because their teeth grow rapidly.

Muskrats prefer quieter water than beavers, but you will occasionally see them on the Snake, more often in adjacent beaver ponds and backwaters. Porcupines live along the river as well, feeding primarily on the cambium of conifers but occasionally on cottonwoods. Marmots appear most frequently in the mountains, where they are commonly called rockchucks. A black melanistic-phase group once lived on the west bank of the Snake at the 4 Lazy F Ranch; we saw them nearly every day from the late 1950s through the mid-1970s.

Red squirrels, also called chickarees and pine squirrels, and northern flying squirrels live in the Snake River bottom, though both are also found in forests at the base of the Tetons. Ground squirrels and chipmunks scurry along the bank, chastising floaters for intruding on their domain. Many people confuse the common golden-mantled ground squirrel with the chipmunk. Chipmunks, however, normally have facial stripes; ground squirrels do not. The common roadside ground squirrel in Jackson Hole is the Uinta, also known as a picket pin or chisler.

Several members of the weasel family live along the Snake, including the winter-white ermine, mink, marten, otter, skunk, and badger. Both the wolverine and the fisher probably live in the wilderness headwaters of the Snake, but both species are relatively rare and normally stay away from human habitation.

None of the weasels are abundant on the Snake, but all are seen several times a season. Mink are small, sleek, and quick with a dark-brown, almost black, coat. Otters live in the water, for the most part, but we sometimes see them on shore, humping along with an almost awkward gait; in the water, they are as fluid as the river itself. Other than the otter, weasels rarely appear in the river; they dwell in the bordering woods. And, incidentally, I have seen more ermine—as weasels in their winter phase are known—while snowshoeing or ski-touring along the Snake in winter than I have seen weasels in their brown-pelted summer phase. Sadly, though, I have seen more weasel roadkills than I have seen weasels alive, winter or summer.

Most people think of badgers as animals of the dry plains, but they also live along the river. I have seen them swim the river, dig out bank-swallow nests, and waddle along the bank, great hairy roly-polies. After a swim, they shake off the water like a shaggy dog. You may occasionally smell skunks; resident dogs tangle with them from time to time to come home carrying the strong odor of their humiliating encounter. They appear in campgrounds, picnic areas, and near residential garbage cans, but due to their nocturnal habits, they are seen along the river relatively rarely.

Whether you are driving through the valley, biking the scenic loop through the potholes, hiking the mountain trails, or floating the Snake River's waters, Jackson Hole offers opportunities to see a vast number of wild creatures in their natural habitat following, for the most part, natural behavioral patterns. Enjoy them but respect their home. They were here long before you and I.

Margaret Altmann

At dusk my first evening in Jackson Hole while walking with friends from Texas, I climbed the path from Jackson Lake Lodge, where I would be working for the summer as employees' recreation director, to the top of Lunch Tree Hill. There John D. Rockefeller Jr. first viewed the Teton Range in the summer of 1926 and decided to help preserve it. As we ascended the hill, I saw a moose in the marsh below the lodge and thoughtlessly yelled, "Look, there's a moose!"

From behind a tree came a deep voice with a heavy German accent: "Shhhhh! Don't scare the animals." Startled and embarrassed, we approached a thickset woman sitting on a little folding stool behind a spotting scope. She wore wool trousers, an alpine hat, and a heavy jacket against the evening cool. Despite her gruff admonition, she had a kindly face, a twinkle in her eye, and a ready smile for us—once she knew we were just ignorant "park savages" needing to be sensitized to the natural world.

This was Margaret Altmann, an ethologist who studied the social behavior of large ungulates: elk, moose, and bison. We talked quietly with her for an hour, while she pointed out other moose, a pair of sandhill cranes, a coyote stalking the cranes, a beaver in the pond below the ridge—until the last light had faded from the sunset sky. Margaret, we learned, knew twenty-two individual moose in that marsh and could identify them by facial or body characteristics. Margaret was fifty-seven at the time, at the peak of her professional life; I was almost twenty-seven—and had met the person who would be my friend and mentor for more than a quarter of a century.

When I began guiding river trips, Margaret took me to task. She did not like the big black pontoons drifting down the Snake with dozens of tourists disturbing the wildlife. As a token of peace, I would share with her my wildlife observations on the river. She often invited me to the Biological Research Station on the west bank of the Snake a mile below the dam, her home for the summer, to listen to scholarly lectures by other wildlife biologists and graduate students. In turn, I often invited her to float with me, but she always rejected my offers.

In 1958 Margaret began teaching at the University of Colorado in Boulder in three different departments: psychology, biology, and sociology. She did not fit readily into any category, but excelled in all three, a true interdisciplinarian. Her summers were spent alone or with a graduate assistant, camping in the backcountry of Yellowstone or the Teton

Margaret Altmann as many remember her, observing wildlife.
Courtesy of Betty Erickson.

Wilderness near the headwaters of the Snake, observing wildlife. This was grizzly country, an area where she might find anything—and she often did, although she concentrated on elk and moose.

Born in Berlin in 1900, Margaret Altmann had been a student of domestic animal behavior at Bonn University where she had earned her Ph.D. in 1928 and where she became one of the outstanding genetic researchers of her time. She carried on a long and lively correspondence with the well-known ethologist Konrad Lorenz. She first visited the United States in 1931 on a Rockefeller Fellowship. When she was selected to work in Adolph Hitler's genetic research program, Margaret left Germany, never to return.

In 1933 she became a resident doctor in the Department of Animal Husbandry at Cornell University and earned another Ph.D., this time in psychobiology, in 1938, the year she became an American citizen. Margaret left Cornell in 1941 to chair the Department of Animal Husbandry and Genetics at Hampton Institute in Virginia for fifteen years. In 1948 she began spending summers in Wyoming, studying communication patterns of wild ungulates.

After more than a decade of invitations to join me on a river trip, Margaret finally accepted—with massive reservations. That evening we saw everything I could imagine—beavers, moose, several species of ducks, elk, sandhill cranes, deer, Canada geese, great blue herons, bald eagles, osprey, porcupines—without disturbing any of the wild creatures. Margaret was an instant convert. Float trips, she realized, gave people an opportunity to see indigenous wildlife in natural surroundings without disturbing it, and it served to educate the general public in appropriate behavior on the river as part of the natural world. After that twilight float, Margaret often recommended our Snake River trips to her friends and students.

An article about Margaret Altmann by David Chiszar and Michael Wertheimer, entitled simply "The Elk Woman," spoke of her "competence, independence, and Teutonic vigor," and suggested that her ideas were thirty years before the times. A professor emeritus at the University of Colorado—where she had taught courses in the social behavior of animal groups in the Department of Psychology until 1969—Margaret died July 6, 1984, twenty-seven years and one month to the day after our initial encounter on Lunch Tree Hill.

Part Two

Floating the River: A Mile-by-Mile Log of the Upper Snake

Key to Maps

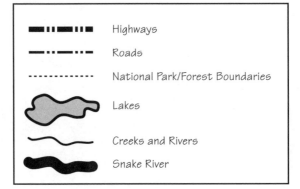

▄▄ ▮▮ ▄▄ ▮▮ ▄▄	Highways
▄▄ ▬·▬·▬ ▄▄	Roads
- - - - - - - - -	National Park/Forest Boundaries
	Lakes
	Creeks and Rivers
	Snake River

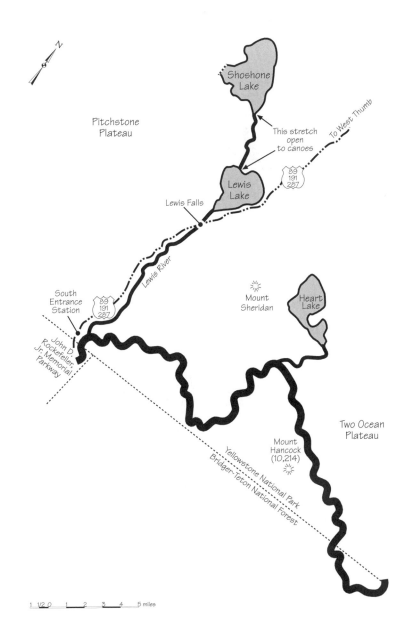

Shoshone
Lake

Pitchstone
Plateau

This stretch
open
to canoes

To West Thumb

Lewis
Lake

89
191
287

Lewis Falls

Lewis River

South
Entrance
Station

89
191
287

John D.
Rockefeller,
Jr. Memorial
Parkway

Mount
Sheridan

Heart
Lake

Two Ocean
Plateau

Mount
Hancock
(10,214)

Yellowstone National Park
Bridger-Teton National Forest

1 1/2 0   1   2   3   4   5 miles

Section 1

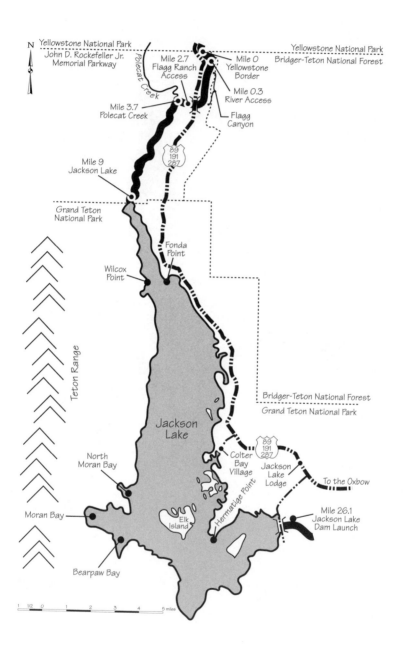

Yellowstone National Park

John D. Rockefeller Jr.
Memorial Parkway

Mile 2.7
Flagg Ranch
Access

Mile 0
Yellowstone
Border

Yellowstone National Park
Bridger-Teton National Forest

Mile 0.3
River Access

Mile 3.7
Polecat Creek

Polecat Creek

Flagg
Canyon

89
191
287

Mile 9
Jackson Lake

Grand Teton
National Park

Fonda
Point

Wilcox
Point

Teton Range

Jackson
Lake

Bridger-Teton National Forest
Grand Teton National Park

North
Moran Bay

Colter
Bay
Village

89
191
287

Jackson
Lake
Lodge

To the Oxbow

Moran Bay

Hermatige Point

Elk
Island

Mile 26.1
Jackson Lake
Dam Launch

Bearpaw Bay

1 1/2 0   1   2   3   4   5 miles

Section 2

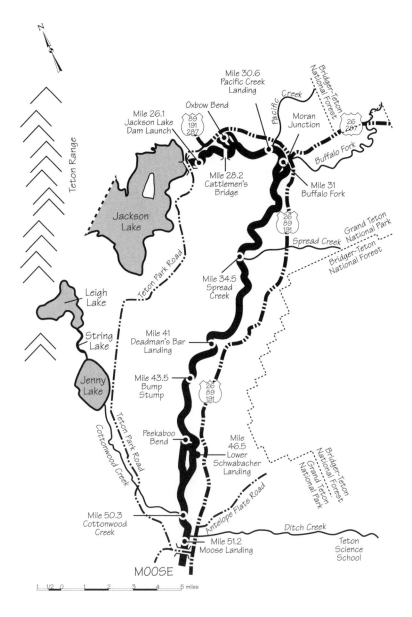

Sections 3 and 4

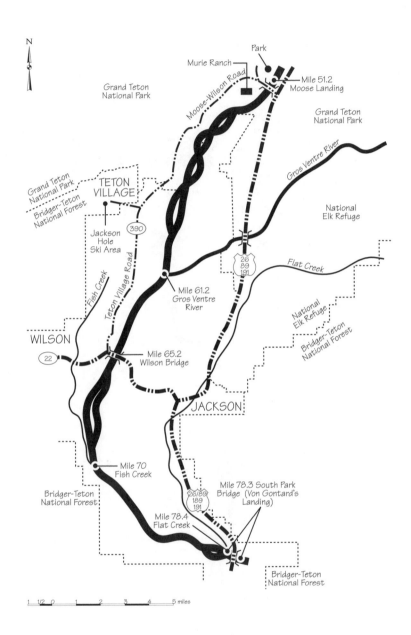

Section 5

114

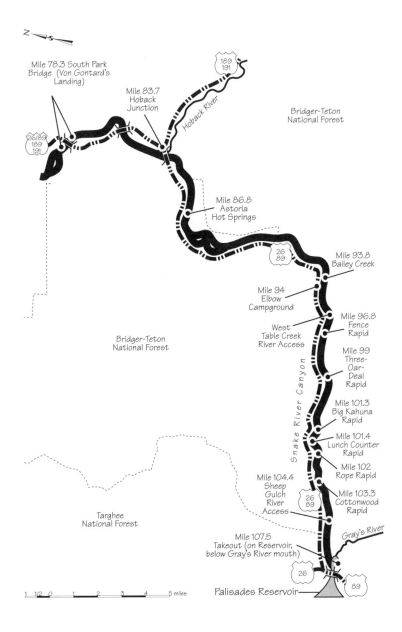

Section 6

River Safety and Etiquette

In spite of the impression you might get from the tragic stories offered by the media, rivers are not inherently dangerous or treacherous if you use common sense and learn how to behave in them, on them, and around them.

Reading a River

To negotiate a river safely, you need to learn to read it: to observe its surface, shorelines, islands, and obvious obstacles, and to understand how to translate these characteristics into appropriate maneuvers in your watercraft, whether it be kayak or canoe, raft or dory—or bullboat. The shoreline and the river bottom may both present various irregularities and obstacles that will dictate where you want your craft to go.

Shoals are simply shallow areas. Sleepers are underwater obstacles, usually broad flat rocks or logs barely underwater that create little surface disturbance but can hang up watercraft if boaters are inattentive. Sweepers are fallen trees hanging over the bank that can—and sometimes do—sweep people out of their watercraft. They are frequently found where the current is strongest. Sawyers are logs with one end anchored on shore or in the river bottom and the other end, usually the treetop, sawing back and forth in the current. (Mark Twain, as a Mississippi riverboat captain, knew sawyers well and used the term for one of his favorite characters, Tom Sawyer.)

Surface disturbances tell the careful and practiced observer a great deal about the obstacles to be contended with. Every surface ripple, hole, or haystack has a meaning and a cause. The river runner must learn to interpret correctly what each one means. Sometimes the disturbance may mean shallow water; another time, the confluence of currents; occasionally, a school of fish or a family of mergansers. Be observant: notice the effect being produced, determine what is causing it, and respond accordingly.

It may be easier to read clear water, because you can see into it

As this wrecked canoe testifies, swift, tricky currents and midstream obstacles present hazards on the Upper Snake, which is primarily a Class I/II river. Photo by Verne Huser.

better, can observe what is causing the surface disturbance. However, many rivers—including the Snake in the spring and early summer—are muddy or cloudy enough to obscure vision. It is important to learn to read turbid water by carefully studying its surface and observing, as best you can, what lies beneath. You need to be able to tell what lies below the surface by careful observation filtered through thoughtful experience.

Look for the current, the flow of water. Normally, it moves downstream, but various obstacles cause eddies, reverse currents that may run upstream along the bank or below an island or a midstream rock. Flotsam, froth, and bubbles often mark the current line. Turbulence marks the eddy line, the dynamic contact zone between downstream flow and reverse currents flowing upstream. Rivers wage a constant battle to reach dynamic equilibrium. When they flow over an obstacle, they hump up, dammed briefly above a rock, log, or ledge, then fall into a depression or hole below it. Downstream water then flows into the hole from whatever direction it can. Powerful upstream currents, racing to fill huge holes below obstacles, create "keepers" that may hold a log or a boat or a person for minutes, hours, even days. Learn to anticipate them, see them well downstream, recognize them for what they are, then avoid them if you can, and hit them head-on if you must.

Look at a river in three different zones as though you were wearing trifocal glasses: what you see—and have to react to—in the next ten yards, what you see in the next hundred yards, what you see in the next thousand yards if you can see that far. If you cannot see well, consider where you might get a better vantage of the river downstream. The current will normally be on the outside of the bend, and it is from the outside of the bend that you can normally get the best and longest downstream view of what lies ahead; rarely can you see around the inside bend.

Keep in mind that on a river, the water moves but the waves stand still because they are created by stationary underwater obstacles. The height of the wave and its shape, the depth of the trough below it, and the location, size, and shape of the whitewater spreading out below it all help to determine the character of unseen obstacles and the nature of the current at any given point. As you float any river, watch what it does to logs or bits of bark in the water. Notice where they go, what they do, how they act as the current plays them—as it will play your craft.

Waves may fill your boat, and their force may pound your hull and veer you off course, but they will not injure you or damage your boat as a rock wall or a jagged, broken tree trunk can. If you have to hit a big wave or a deep hole, hit it head-on, at a right angle to its axis, but try to avoid waves as much as possible.

Keep in mind that as water levels rise, the current increases in velocity and the direction of flow may change as higher river levels find different routes through islands and obstacles. When currents change in direction and velocity, they create subtle side currents and lateral flows that have to be incorporated into the equation.

Only careful observation and experience on the river can teach you to read water. Some people come by it naturally, but seat-of-the-pants intuition is not everything. Flowing water follows certain physical laws. You do not have to know the laws, but you do have to be aware of their effects and learn to interpret and apply your understanding and knowledge to keep your craft under control and you and your passengers out of harm's way.

What To Do If You Find Yourself in the River

Your priorities are	Your problems might be
yourself	hyperventilation
your companions	entrapment
your craft	being crushed
your gear	hypothermia

Posted at the most popular launch site at West Table Creek in the Snake River Canyon, this U.S. Forest Service sign offers a warning that should not be taken lightly. Photo by Verne Huser.

If you find yourself in the water, stay calm and assess your situation. It will vary with the craft and conditions. If you have fallen out of a craft, it is one thing; if the craft has capsized, it is another; but in either case, let your personal flotation device do its job of floating you on your back.

If you are floating in the current and are not under a watercraft, skull with your hands to position yourself facing downstream (so you can see where you are going and what obstacles may be approaching), pull your legs to the surface (so you can ward off any obstacles and so they do not get caught in underwater rocks or logs).

In cold water, you will want to get out as quickly as possible, then get dry and warm, and you probably cannot do either in the water. The water temperature will dictate the answer to the question, do I stay with the craft or go for shore?

Experienced river runners, such as these race contestants, take safety very seriously. Both paddlers are wearing PFDs, and one uses the swamped canoe for extra flotation, while extending a paddle to the swimmer in the current. Photo by Verne Huser.

If you go for shore, choose a shore where safety lies, not a shore against a cliff opposite the road, where others would have difficulty reaching you. Try not to float into a serious logjam, and do not try to stand in fast-moving water: you might get your foot wedged between rocks, and the current could force you underwater and hold you there. Any kind of entrapment should be avoided.

Should you be caught beneath a raft, either one that remains upright or one that has flipped upside down, push off (toward the river bottom) to get out from under the bulky craft. Your PFD may be holding you in a position that does not allow you to breathe.

Should a dory flip, watch out for the gunwale so that it does not hit you as it capsizes. In the water, try to move upstream of the capsized dory to avoid being pinned against a rock by the heavy craft, made heavier by the water in it and the force of the current against it.

In a kayak, you will try to Eskimo roll to an upright position, but if you fail, go for a swim. Try to stay with your craft as it provides flotation for you. Be careful not to become entrapped in the craft should it be swept into a sweeper or logjam or lodged between a low-lying log and the water.

In a canoe you may swamp without capsizing. You may still be able to control the craft with paddles, but it may be best to try to swim it to shore. As with a kayak, most canoes will offer flotation to assist the paddlers. The same is true of a raft or any inflatable craft.

If someone falls out of a canoe, the canoe will most likely capsize, but it will still float. The critical element is not to be caught between the canoe and a rock downstream, a situation that could crush a swimmer. Try to get upstream of any hard-hulled craft to prevent being crushed.

The specific situation dictates the best action to take, but stay calm, do not panic, and devise a plan with the help of your traveling companions. Panic may lead to hyperventilation (extremely deep or rapid breaths that overoxygenate the blood), and losing too much body heat may lead to hypothermia. Entrapment or being crushed between a craft and a rock can be deadly. Avoid each possibility and treat the eventuality appropriately.

Keep your priorities in mind: first, yourself; then the other members of your party; third, your craft; and finally, the gear floating about in the water. A man drowned in the Snake River Canyon several years ago while trying to recover a flotation pillow after he had made it safely ashore.

Safety and Etiquette

It should go without saying that booze and boats do not mix any better than drinking and driving; of course, illegal drugs have no business on the river. I object to tobacco use as well: discarding butts *is* littering, and the juice leaching from them into the river, in high enough concentrations, can kill fish.

The single most important safety item is the personal flotation device, or PFD as the Coast Guard calls it, more commonly known as a life vest or life jacket. It is neither vest nor jacket, but it can save your life—if you wear it, if you wear it properly, and if it fits. I always wear my PFD, even in flat water, as much as an example to others as for my own safety.

Although it may seem counterintuitive, there are times when the safest thing to do is take off your PFD: if you are trapped in a keeper, removing your PFD may be the only way to get swept out of the hydraulic; if you are caught beneath an overturned boat and your PFD keeps you afloat so that you cannot escape, you may have to remove it; if your PFD straps are caught on a snag or part of the boat, you may have to slip out of it to save your life—but those are rare exceptions to the rule: *always* wear your PFD.

River etiquette includes showing consideration for animal inhabitants.
The immature bald eagle seen here seems to be driving home the point.
Courtesy of Dick Barker.

In general, avoid obstacles such as sawyers, sleepers, and sweepers, and especially avoid any obstacle that might cause entrapment,
the most dangerous situation on the river. Entrapment occurs when
you are caught, trapped, or held above or underwater by the current's playing against you or your craft in a dangerous manner.
Within my memory are many accidents that might have had hap-
pier outcomes if their victims had reacted differently: the Boy Scout
who drowned when his canoe wrapped around a bridge piling with
him trapped in it by the force of the water breaking over it; the man
who was swept through the branches of a submerged tree and became trapped underwater after his raft flipped; the kayaker who
was forced under a log by the swift current.

Avoid obstacles that might damage people or equipment, or that
might capsize a craft or send people into the water where other
mishaps may befall them. Avoid confrontations with wild animals,
primarily bear, bison, and moose. In high water avoid getting too
close to trees on the river's edge that have been undercut by the current and might topple into the river and fall across a craft or block a
channel.

Because most river accidents actually occur off the river, take care
when stepping on slick or loose rocks at the river edge and when
launching or landing as you enter the craft or go ashore. Stay alert

to avoid falling onto sharp rocks or being stabbed by limbs or logs. Although no poisonous plants or snakes exist in Jackson Hole, white-faced hornets do, and hornets can cause painful stings, even death from anaphylactic shock. White-faced hornets built a nest one summer in a tree that overhung a swift channel; guides had to be careful to avoid it, an unusual river hazard.

If you float a river, you should know something about the river, the craft, and the people with you. Knowledge about the flow level and distance to the next takeout dictates what you bring with you, how much food and water and clothing you should have along. Two of the most frequent problems among novice river runners are dehydration (heat exhaustion) and hypothermia (heat loss). Neither beer nor carbonated sodas provide adequate water to prevent dehydration; in fact, they both increase dehydration. If you get wet on the river, especially if your clothes get wet, you may lose more body heat than you can afford to and still retain all your faculties and functions.

Windstorms are rare in midsummer, but thunderstorms occur frequently. It is in the segment of river below Deadman's Bar that most people encounter them, for the storms usually hit in the afternoon, especially in the late afternoon, when the most popular trip on the river is under way. People floating the twenty-mile stretch from Pacific Creek to Moose encounter storms on the latter half of their trip after lunch; and evening floaters who launch after 5 P.M. often catch storms that have been building all afternoon. Commercial companies carry raincoats for their passengers, and private users who have any sense carry them as well.

The storms produce a lot of lightning and occasional hail. Most lightning hits either in the mountains or on high points of the outwash plain (moraines, for example). But bear in mind that although the river is the lowest point in the valley, it has big trees along the bank to serve as lightning rods.

Storms on the river can be frightening, but I must admit that some of my most memorable trips have occurred during violent storms. Moose go wild with hailstones falling, running hither and yon, seeking shelter, and a pair of sandhill cranes once flew so low over the river they had to separate to miss my boat, flying around the ends at a distance of no more than twenty feet. I have noticed that beavers respect thunderstorms, seldom appearing when lightning strikes or thunder roars anywhere near the river.

Approaching storms create fantastic cloud patterns on the river and over the mountains. Occasionally, storms leave new snow on

Violent thunderstorms occur on the Snake River, bringing lightning, high wind, rain, and hail. Floaters need to be prepared for hypothermia. You are generally safer on the river than on shore in such storms. Photo by Verne Huser.

the higher peaks, even in midsummer, and every few summers we get a good snowfall on the river itself. Over the years I have seen snow on the river every month from April through October. I usually do not float the Snake between November and March, but Frank Ewing and I once canoed it with Dave Demaree on the Audubon Christmas Bird Count in mid-December.

Names become important during emergencies on the river, and emergencies do occur every summer—more often with private groups than with commercial trips, but even pros occasionally run into trouble. Canoeists frequently have problems on the Snake River, especially in the swift, highly braided segments between Pacific Creek and Moose.

The Park Service provides maps with standardized names to river runners who register, as all are required to do, for a Snake River float trip. The fee is modest, and the visitor contact provides the rangers an opportunity to distribute their important information about the river.

If you decide to book a scenic guided trip rather than row or paddle yourself, here are some things to consider. Responsible river guides not only know the river and how to get people safely to the takeout, but also know the Park Service rules and regulations as well as the basic principles of river etiquette, and they practice them. They know basic first aid and stay in practice (they are required by the National Park Service to be Red Cross certified). They are familiar with basic rescue procedures and know the nearest vehicle access points on both sides of the river—and they know the standard river names.

Above and beyond the essential skills for getting people safely down the river, responsible guides need to be well informed about the entire area. Too many licensed river guides seem interested only in getting their paying passengers to the takeout as quickly as possible. They cheat their clients out of the relaxing experience of floating down the river at the pace of the current. By rowing downstream, irresponsible guides create congestion on the river, reducing the park visitors' opportunity to enjoy the solitude inherent in the river experience. Furthermore, such guides impair their passengers' chances of seeing wildlife; the action of rowing is more likely to frighten the birds and animals along the river than would simply going with the flow. A *float* trip should be what the name suggests: floating along the surface of the river at the current's pace.

Good river guides know the geology, history, and folklore of the valley; they know the flora, fauna, and people of the area. They should be able to recommend off-river excursions, good restaurants, the best places to find wildlife off the river, and even, perhaps, the most scenic route to Salt Lake City, Idaho Falls, or Yellowstone. They should know something about off-river and off-season activities: skiing, hunting and fishing, snowmobiling, climbing, hiking the mountain trails, horseback riding, and scenic flights.

Good river guides know how to keep passengers dry and well informed, entertained and comfortable on the water. They know how to deal with people who may be apprehensive about being out in the wilds, perhaps for the first time, without a car window between them and the natural world. They know how to help their clients understand and appreciate the experience. And they know how to take care of the river.

Section 1

In Yellowstone National Park

The true source of the Snake River is a spring a few hundred yards south of Yellowstone National Park's southern boundary, but the headwater Snake flows for many miles through the park: northwest between Barlow Peak (9,622 feet) and Mount Hancock (10,214 feet), paralleling Big Game Ridge, then west to its meeting with the Heart River. From the Heart River confluence, it swings south, almost reaching the park's southern boundary, loops northwest again, then west at Snake Hot Springs, and finally southwest to its confluence with Lewis River near another ancient thermal area within sight of the South Entrance Station of Yellowstone National Park on U.S. Highway 89/287.

Two major sources in the park, along with Lewis Lake, supply water to the Upper Snake: Heart Lake Geyser Basin and Shoshone Geyser Basin. The Heart Lake Geyser Basin, discovered in 1870 by members of the Washburn-Doane Expedition, was rediscovered in 1871 by army captain J. W. Barlow. (The Upper Snake River was for a time named Barlow Creek.) Lewis Lake, which lies along the main highway through Yellowstone National Park, is joined by the Lewis River to Shoshone Lake in the Shoshone Geyser Basin, located in the southern interior of Yellowstone National Park. The Lewis River continues below Lewis Lake, draining both basins into the Snake.

While the Shoshone and Heart Lake Geyser Basins flow into the main Snake (known to most Idahoans as the South Fork and the tributary this book covers), the park's wild Bechler Corner offers its water to Henry's Fork of the Snake southwest of the park. The Pitchstone Plateau rises high above and south of Shoshone Lake, west of Lewis Lake. Falls River flows off the southern aspect of this volcanic plateau, the Bechler River off its western slopes in the most spectacular concentrations of waterfalls in the park.

As you travel by highway through southern Yellowstone National Park, the Lewis River appears in three guises along the road between the South Entrance and West Thumb: the spectacular

A tiny tributary joins Mountain Ash Creek, a Snake River source stream, at Union Falls in the southwest corner of Yellowstone National Park.
Photo by Verne Huser.

twenty-nine-foot cascade known as Lewis Falls just above the highway bridge; a placid stream below the bridge, meandering through a moose meadow; and a shimmering, sun-reflecting river dropping deeper and deeper into a basaltic gorge, then disappearing from sight as it wends its way to a confluence with the Snake.

Lewis River and Lewis Lake are the only aspects of the Snake River that still retain the name originally bestowed upon it by members of the Lewis and Clark Expedition, who—more than a thousand miles downstream and nearly two hundred years ago, at the confluence of the Clearwater with the Snake in 1805—named the river for Meriwether Lewis. To them it was the Lewis River, but the name never caught on—except for this relatively small appendage within Yellowstone National Park.

The only river segment in the park on which boating is allowed, Lewis River between Lewis and Shoshone Lakes lies out of sight, unknown to most park visitors. To reach Lewis River you may hike or ride horseback several miles west into the backcountry or paddle

A trio of river otters plays in the shallow water of Lewis River during midwinter in southern Yellowstone National Park.

across Lewis Lake from the lakeshore along U.S. 89/191/287 where ample parking exists. Often windy, especially in the afternoon, Lewis Lake offers a sometimes-treacherous crossing; four- and five-foot waves are not uncommon. I have on more than one occasion simply led my canoe—like a well-trained dog—along the north-shore beach, while my paddling partner used my aluminum pole to keep the bow of the canoe angled out into the lake as the strong wind constantly attempted to beach it.

Crossing the lake by canoe, headed for the western shoreline, you will eventually see a broad bay breaking away into the north-western interior like a thumb leading away from an open hand. That bay narrows to the northwest and gradually shallows, leading into what fishermen call "the aquarium," a long channel fifteen to twenty feet deep with water so clear you can see all the fish and plants between the surface and the bottom, a natural aquarium where generations of anglers have found good fishing.

Motorized crafts are forbidden on Lewis River, which is difficult to differentiate from the narrowing arm of the lake except for official signs that make it clear. The aquarium snakes northward, shallow-ing and constricting until you see the end of the arm and wonder what becomes of the river. Suddenly you notice a gap in the rock to the left: the river flows quietly into the aquarium through a narrow gate in the lichen-covered rock.

Above the gate the river moves slowly, still clear and deep, not as narrow as the gap nor as wide as the aquarium, continuing to shal-

A lone canoeist heads into Lewis River from Shoshone Lake in Yellowstone's southern region, a major source of Snake River water.

low gradually until it breaks out of braids and meanders, and becomes a cold mountain stream. Along the shoreline you may see moose, deer, elk, bear. Fish flash through the clear water, while eagles and osprey search the riffles for a meal. Stellar jays, gray jays, and robins jeer. A black-headed grosbeak sings from a high hidden perch, a Townsend's solitaire pipes its song from a single topmost spare, and a squirrel scurries away, chattering its displeasure at being disturbed.

Soon the flow, too swift to paddle or pole against, requires the canoeist to line the craft upstream, a labor frustrated by fallen timber and frequent sawyers. I simply wade through the water, only inches deep at this point, in my hard-soled wet boots or old running shoes with wool socks on my feet: the water is cold, but, properly dressed, a canoeist can brave the current and force the canoe upstream slowly, steadily to the outlet of Shoshone Lake where Lewis River actually begins.

Shoshone Lake, the heart of the Shoshone Geyser Basin, lies in a verdant landscape warmed by numerous geysers in wilderness guarded by distance from trailheads. Hikers and horseback riders in summer and cross-country skiers in winter visit the basin in small numbers to camp and observe wildlife, virtually every species present in the park including bison, grizzly bear, the biggest moose I have seen in Yellowstone, Canada geese, and wolves (one of the recently transplanted wolves, a pregnant female, was scalded to death her first winter in the park in one of the many thermal pools here).

I have visited the Shoshone Geyser Basin only three times, each time by a different means, each delightful in its own way: on cross-country skis in winter, on horseback in late summer, and by canoe in midsummer. Unique thermal features decorate Shoshone Geyser Basin: tiny streamlets of scalding water lined with algal strings, their colors specific to the temperatures they can tolerate; small, nearly round potholes bubbling with steaming water; unseasonal flowers blooming in the microclimates created by the hot water; and wildlife attracted to the warmer zone in winter and lush, well-watered vegetation in summer.

The canoe trip back to Lewis Lake simply reverses the upstream route, but now you are paddling with the current, an easier activity but just as likely to produce unique wildlife observations because the downstream trip may be quieter. Though the canoe trip from Lewis Lake to Shoshone Lake may take almost two hours, the return trip will require less than half that time.

A trailhead north of Lewis Lake and on the east side of the highway leads to Heart Lake, a natural reservoir that catches the snowmelt of the other main Snake tributary. Members of the 1876-1877 Doane Expedition crossed the Continental Divide from West Thumb Bay on Yellowstone Lake to the Heart Lake Geyser Basin during their late-fall exploration of the Upper Snake, and found the south end of the lake frozen and the river below the lake, now known as Heart River, too shallow to float. Using mules, they dragged the boat over the rough, rocky streambed, negotiating only three miles a day and badly damaging the boat's bottom.

Below what they called Barlow Creek (now the Upper Snake), they found water enough to float the boat and continued their exploration downstream. Doane declared Lewis River, flowing twice the volume of the stream they had followed, "the true source of the Snake," but he was wrong; in his journal, in fact, he states at least three different times that this or that tributary is the true source of the Snake, and he never gets it right. The true source of the Snake was discovered in 1971 by a pair of Jackson Hole explorers, Paul Lawrence and park ranger Joe Shellenburger; through the efforts of Dave Love, the source of the Snake now appears correctly on USGS maps of the area. Eventually, the Doane party reached Jackson Lake, which had not yet frozen, and followed its western shore to the lake's outlet, now the site of Jackson Lake Dam.

Relatively few people know the Snake in Yellowstone because much of it flows through wild country without trails and where no boats are allowed. Even the Snake River (South Boundary) Trail along the lower segments of the river in the park lies across the Snake from the road and is impossible to access without a long hike up Arizona Creek in the Teton Wilderness or a boat to cross the Snake—unless you are willing to wade or swim the river, a dangerous activity most of the year. A ford indicated on some maps may be valid in late summer or early fall, but I would not count on it; few people do, one reason this part of the park remains so isolated and little traveled. Most people first see the Upper Snake from the road at the South Entrance.

The summer of 1973 my wife and I spent ten days on horseback exploring Yellowstone from the Bechler Corner to Heart Lake, then followed the Snake out of the park, fording its midsummer flow a final time below Huckleberry Mountain (9,615 feet) in what is now the John D. Rockefeller Jr. Memorial Parkway. Elk were everywhere on the Upper Snake and bird life abundant, especially western tanagers. Flowing through steep country for the most part, the Upper Snake suffered considerable fire damage the summer of 1988, but the vegetation is returning through natural plant succession patterns, following a centuries-old process.

Leaving Yellowstone National Park, the Snake is on its way to Jackson Hole. It is possible to hike from the South Entrance Station less than a mile along the west bank of the Snake to the mouth of the Lewis River; many fly fishermen do. The river has created a broad meadow there, a popular place for elk to graze at dawn and dusk, and a good place to observe what rivers do in relatively flat terrain: meander between banks, thread through islands, leave piles of driftwood at the heads of islands, undercut and overflow banks, build gravel bars, and deposit silt wherever eddies slow the current.

The South Entrance Station segment of the Snake represents a transition zone for the river dropping out of the steeper country and spreading out in the broad valley before diving into a much narrower canyon bound by hard-rock walls. Few people other than fishermen bother to get out of their cars at the South Entrance Station, but there is a small picnic area nearby and parking spaces for a respite from the road and tourist traffic—a fine place to get to know the Snake.

Section 2 (26 miles)

Yellowstone National Park to Jackson Lake Dam

At dawn or dusk look eastward from the Yellowstone South Entrance Station, and you may see elk feeding in a meadow along the Snake River as it meanders through an ancient geyser basin immediately opposite the mouth of Lewis River less than a mile from the park's south boundary. This meadow may be the site of the Doane Expedition's camp in November 1876. I have found no evidence of lodgepole stumps there, but Doane's journal suggests that his party stopped there to recaulk their boat and cut tipi poles before entering the steep-walled segment known today as Flagg Canyon. Most of their newly trimmed poles broke against the rocky canyon wall as they continued their trip.

I have paddled upstream from the launch site a few hundred yards south of the Yellowstone South Entrance Station to the park boundary and, landing on the left bank (east side), hiked the South Boundary Trail to the steaming geyser basin filled with wildflowers in early spring: blue camas, yellow monkey flowers, yellow-and-magenta shooting stars, and deep-purple larkspur.

Boating is prohibited on Yellowstone rivers with the single exception of Lewis River between Lewis and Shoshone Lakes, but the launch site at a turnout and picnic area within sight of the Yellowstone South Entrance Station provides access to an exciting stretch of the Upper Snake just south of the park boundary. There harlequin ducks and water ouzels appear in the spring, and both bald eagles and osprey fish nearby. The canyon stretch, less than two miles long, offers six-, eight-, ten-foot waves in a canyon no more than forty- to fifty-feet wide during spring snowmelt runoff, an exhilarating run in a small inflatable boat.

In late summer and early fall, when the water is lower, this stretch has a peaceful quality, ideal for poling a canoe or paddling a small raft and viewing wildlife. Full of whitefish, this reach is

The Snake River flows through the narrow, rocky Flagg Canyon just downstream from Yellowstone National Park's South Entrance. After cutting tipi poles in their camp across from the mouth of the Lewis River, members of the 1876 Doane Expedition broke most of them on these volcanic walls. Photo by Verne Huser.

especially popular with gulls and white pelicans. Beavers appear in early evening at the canyon's lower end near the mouth of Sheffield Creek, a favorite fishing hole. There a massive beaver marsh occupies the left bank just above a big bend to the right (west) above the U.S. 89/191/287 bridge over the Snake. A river access point lies on the right bank just below the bridge at Flagg Ranch, a takeout for the canyon stretch, a put-in for the next segment, and a good place to watch wildlife and catch both whitefish and trout.

The entire river route from Yellowstone's South Entrance to the lake and the northern boundary of Grand Teton National Park has the protection of the National Park Service. This narrow corridor between the parks became the John D. Rockefeller Jr. Memorial Parkway in 1972 to commemorate Rockefeller's vital role in helping to preserve the whole area. The nearly twenty-four-thousand-acre parkway connects the two parks, allowing unrestricted migration of species between Yellowstone and Grand Teton, one of the first such corridors in the nation to be implemented.

Flagg Ranch, named for a flagpole in nearby Soldier Meadow, which served as a military post when the army administered Yellowstone (until 1917), has had a disjointed recent history. Its buildings—including a restaurant, gift shop, hotel, cabins, service station, and associated businesses—have burned to the ground on more than one occasion. In recent years the facilities, which now include a ranger station and campground, have been moved north away from the river, but some old buildings remain. A park ranger friend of mine once wintered at Flagg Ranch, enjoying not only the solitude of a season in the snow, but the companionship of a resident pine marten that lived in the chaotic attic of the main building, long since burned down.

Launching at the Flagg Ranch access point enables you to run the seven-mile stretch of Snake River to Jackson Lake. When the lake reaches its highest level (6,772 feet), this trip is reduced by two miles as the reservoir reaches into the river delta, creating flat water on the lower reaches of the drowned river. In any case the trip requires at least three additional miles of paddling or rowing (or powerboating) on Jackson Lake to reach the takeout at Fonda Point in the Lizard Creek Campground. Fonda Point is named for ranger John Fonda, who died after falling through the ice the winter of 1960 on a routine winter patrol across the frozen lake. Wilcox Point across the lake commemorates Gale Wilcox who died in the same accident.

Although the Flagg Ranch–to–Jackson Lake stretch may seem short, and though it ends on a reservoir, it has much to recommend it: rare views of the Teton Range from the north, good fishing, a better-than-average chance to see wildlife in a natural setting, and a true wilderness experience. The river there is usually clear and relatively shallow after a brief spurt of turbid water during spring snowmelt, and it flows through an area full of wildlife: mink, muskrats, moose, beavers, and bear as well as sandhill cranes, bald eagles, white pelicans, and several species of ducks.

Fishing may be best at lower water levels and in the tributary streams: Polecat and Glade Creeks on the right bank, Quarter and Dime Creeks on the left, where a former Forest Service campground has been abandoned. The marsh harbors a wide variety of colorful nesting birds in summer.

The river flows almost due west for a mile, swift and clear, braiding into two or three channels—it changes from year to year—as it approaches a big bend to the south where Polecat Creek enters from the right. High-water overflow channels on the left bank create a marsh where beavers abound, along with evidence of their handiwork on lodgepole pines, the only mature trees around. Beavers do indeed feed on conifers when evergreens constitute the only trees in the neighborhood.

The river flows almost due south for the next five miles, again braiding and splitting into shallow, narrow channels. Logjams decorate the sand and gravel bars, occasionally forcing a brief portage or a channel change. I have frequently seen elk, especially early in the morning or late in the afternoon, in this vicinity, and I once surprised a sow black bear with three cubs at a bend of the river: the sow gave me one look, then woofed to her cubs, and they went splashing across the channel and into the woods. Sandhill cranes enjoy the isolation of the bordering marshes, and bald eagles fish from riverbank trees.

As the river approaches Jackson Lake west of Steamboat Mountain (7,872 feet), bald eagle and osprey nests—and the birds themselves—appear in trees killed by rising reservoir waters. Huge rafts of ducks, geese, and other waterfowl, and occasionally white pelicans and trumpeter swans, frequent the upper (north) end of the impoundment. At high lake levels you can paddle, row, or motor across drowned meanders to shorten the trip, but windy days can make the crossing difficult, even dangerous.

I almost died on the lake one day: on a solo open-canoe trip I reached it during a gathering storm that generated forty-mile-per-hour up-lake winds. Waves four- and five-feet high pounded me into the left bank as I pushed along with a twelve-foot wooden pole. For every push I would advance the canoe about three feet, then have the canoe blown against the bank by the fierce wind. If I tried to stop for a rest, the canoe would be battered against the logs and rocks gathered at the shoreline, threatening to capsize the craft. My arms were leaden, my legs quivering, but I knew if I did not keep pushing off the shoreline, I would never get to Fonda Point. With a strong river current, I made 5.5 miles the first hour, then hit slack water and made only 2.5 miles the second hour, and, once on the open lake, only 1 mile per hour. What a relief when I finally arrived at the takeout in the midst of a thunderstorm—even though it drenched me, terrified me with lightning, and bombarded me with hail. To say the least, I was grateful to be off the reservoir.

Archaeological sites along the upper reaches of the artificial Jackson Lake, excavated during reconstruction work on the dam in the 1980s when water levels were held near the lake's natural levels, suggest summer occupancy by prehistoric native peoples. High elevation, severe winter cold, and migration of wildlife species out of the valley were enough to discourage later Native Americans from settling permanently in the area, but they apparently hunted and fished during warmer months, preserving meat and gathering natural foods to store for the winter. Tradition suggests that enemy tribes abided by a general truce in the valley of the Upper Snake during their summer visits. Such tribes included Bannock, Blackfeet, Crow, perhaps Gros Ventre, certainly Shoshone, and others as well. Nez Perce and Flatheads are known to have attended the nearby fur rendezvous.

Jackson Lake serves as a barrier to most visitors to Grand Teton National Park, few of whom explore the west shore of the lake, which enjoys wilderness protection. The rarely maintained trails on the west side of the lake can be reached only by boat—or extremely long hikes. Powerboats and rental canoes can be found at Leek's Marine, Colter Bay, and Signal Mountain Lodge, or, with the proper park permit, you can launch your own craft to access the west shore, which is the one Doane and his intrepid men explored the late fall of 1876.

A series of loop trails access the northern Teton Range and connect to Forest Service trails in the Jedediah Smith Wilderness west of the Tetons' hydrologic divide. A primary trailhead lies at the small bay into which both Owl Creek and Webb Creek flow—directly across the lake from Fonda Point and immediately north of Wilcox Point, less than a mile by canoe. One of the wildest portions of Grand Teton National Park, this northern wilderness includes Berry Creek, Owl Creek, and the well-watered Moose Basin. One of my favorite one-day hikes, the lower loop west up Owl Creek, north along Berry Creek, then back east and south behind Haram Hill, offers wildflowers galore, wild country, and opportunities to see mule deer, elk, sandhill cranes, even grizzly bears as well as forest-dwelling birds such as the colorful western tanager.

Numerous Forest Service wilderness routes branch off the Berry Creek trail west of the divide over Jackass Pass (8,460 feet) and historic Conant Pass, including routes along the various forks of Boone Creek, Conant Creek, Grizzly Creek, North and South Bitch Creeks, and Badger Creek in the Jedediah Smith Wilderness in Targhee National Forest. Conant Pass lies at the head of Berry Creek, the route that many historians believe John Colter followed the winter of 1807-1808 when he is reputed to have discovered Jackson Hole.

The main highway (U.S. 89/191/287) runs along the eastern shore of Jackson Lake, marked by several scenic turnouts. A trailhead near the mouth of Arizona Creek leads serious hikers and autumn elk hunters into the Teton Wilderness, an area of abundant, varied wildlife, supreme solitude, and magnificent views of the Teton Range.

A few miles south of Arizona Creek is Leek's Lodge and Marina, a private inholding on the lake within the park boundaries, providing boating opportunities, meals, and lodging. It originally served as a hunting and fishing lodge for Stephen N. Leek who homesteaded the land south of Jackson and played an integral role in the establishment of the National Elk Refuge.

Across the lake from Leek's Lodge and Marina and a few miles south of the Moose Creek–Owl Creek trail complex on the lake's west shore is Waterfalls Canyon. The canyon boasts spectacular and isolated Columbine Cascades and Wilderness Falls, the highest waterfall in the park, which can be seen from the main highway and from Colter Bay. No trail violates this pristine watercourse, but hardy hikers can bushwhack their way into the upper basin at the foot of the falls. With a bit of careful route finding and scrambling, you can climb above the falls to the tiny alpine lake nestled into the ridge that joins Eagles Nest Peak to Doane Peak (11,355 feet).

Two miles south of Waterfalls Canyon lies Moran Bay. North Moran Creek, its north fork originating from a small, permanent snowfield on the upper south face of Doane Peak, joins its south fork in Snowshoe Canyon, which embraces Rolling Thunder Mountain (10,908 feet) behind Eagles Nest Peak (11,258 feet), and flows into Jackson Lake at the north shore of Moran Bay. Here Doane and his men tested the echo chamber of nearby Moran Canyon, one of the range's deepest, wildest canyons that flows into the bay from the west.

Its south wall is marked by three small glaciers (Triple Glaciers) on Mount Moran, named for the artist Thomas Moran, who first painted the Yellowstone and Grand Teton area. Though few peaks in the northern part of the Teton Range rise above 11,000 feet, the higher central peaks of the range begin at Mount Moran (12,605 feet), found immediately above Moran Bay. Two major glaciers decorate its rocky east face: Skillet Glacier, which resembles a large frying pan facing northeast, and Falling Ice Glacier facing southeast.

Wilderness Falls in Waterfall Canyon, a prominent feature on the west bank of Jackson Lake, beckons few visitors to the isolated wilderness across the lake from the main highway. Photo by Verne Huser.

The Snake as it appeared in the early 1900s, flowing into Jackson Hole. The river meandered widely, forming oxbows and marshes that were drowned when Jackson Lake Dam raised the level of the natural lake by some forty feet. Courtesy of the Jackson Hole Historical Society.

From Moran Bay, Elk Island lies two miles immediately to the east. East of Elk Island lies the Colter Bay Complex. As part of Mission 66, a major effort to upgrade visitor facilities within the national park system, the development at Colter Bay sprang up in the late 1950s and early 1960s on the ragged eastern shore of Jackson Lake just across from the base of Mount Moran, offering a spectacular view of the park's fifth-highest—and most massive—peak. The Colter Bay development has become a favorite among park visitors. A major marina exists there as well as cabins, stores, a cafeteria, and a visitors' center that houses the Rockefeller collection of Plains Indians artifacts.

Due east of Leek's Lodge and northeast of Colter Bay rises Pilgrim Mountain (8,274 feet) in the Teton Wilderness. The bushwhacking hike to its summit offers one of the finest views of Jackson Lake and the Teton Range I have seen. It has been one of my favorite hikes since my first summer in the area, but today it is encompassed by an expanding grizzly bear habitat, and I now hike there with great caution and a few friends. The road to the base of Pilgrim Mountain spurs north off the main highway (U.S. 89/191/287) between Colter Bay and Jackson Lake Lodge. I recommend the hike

The newly completed Jackson Lake Dam was a curiosity to visitors in the 1920s. The town of Moran in the background was thriving at that time, but was removed in the late 1950s, allowing the area to revert to a more natural setting in keeping with its new national park status. Courtesy of the Jackson Hole Historical Society.

for great wildflowers in early summer and for spectacular views of Waterfalls Canyon west of the lake and of the whole panorama of peaks west of Jackson Lake.

At Hermitage Point a popular, partially paved trail from Colter Bay offers park visitors some of the best low-level views of Jackson Lake, Mount Moran, and the entire Teton Range. To the southwest the irregular south shore of Jackson Lake is cut deeply by Bearpaw and Spalding Bays, separated by Deadman's Point. Spalding Bay marks the southern-most arm of the lake as the south shoreline begins to bend northeast toward the lake's natural outlet—and the dam. Signal Mountain Lodge and Boat Ramp are about a mile southwest of the lake outlet and dam.

Originally, Jackson Lake was a natural impoundment, created by a moraine deposited when a major valley glacier retreated. The moraine served as a barrier that diverted the Snake to the northeast and forced it into its present pattern, flowing in a loop around Signal Mountain. To augment its natural storage capacity for human use, a dam was built and the lake enlarged. The first dam, built in 1906, was a simple log-crib structure three feet high and filled with rocks, but when it washed out in a 1910 flood, a new earth-fill dam

Waters backing up behind the Jackson Lake Dam drowned acres of trees. Winds blew the resulting driftwood to the north end of Jackson Lake, which blocked access to the lake and created a fire hazard. Courtesy of the Jackson Lake Historical Society.

was constructed by the Bureau of Reclamation in 1910-1911, raising the lake ten feet.

In 1914 the Bureau of Reclamation began building the present dam. This concrete structure at the natural outlet of Jackson Lake was completed in 1916, and raised the lake level roughly forty feet. The reservoir capacity has thus been increased to 847,000 acre-feet. For years after the dam was built, massive rafts of dead timber covered much of the lake and upper (northern) lakeshore.

Water stored in the artificial impoundment belongs to Idaho irrigators, who also tried—but failed—to build dams in the southwest (Bechler) corner of Yellowstone National Park in the 1920s. When the National Park Service refused to allow dams to be built within the park, the irrigators tried to delete land from the park through congressional action to allow their water-development projects to be built, but again they failed.

Within a six-mile radius of the Jackson Lake outlet where the dam now rations water to the Snake River, most tourist facilities in Grand Teton National Park exist: a hotel and cabins, marinas and campgrounds, restaurants and bars, service stations and horse corrals, back roads and trails. During summer months the population of the park rises to several thousand people per night, a heavy impact upon so small an area, but by concentrating the impact, the National Park Service and its concessionaires have been able to preserve most of the park in its natural state.

The town of Moran, once located below the dam on the left bank of the river, was moved in 1959 to allow the area to return to a more natural state. The town essentially disappeared, its reincarnation hidden away behind a ridge of trees near the park's east entrance.

The wildlife remains. The fishing is good. The park visitors are happy for the most part. The lake supports sailboats, powerboats, and a few canoes as well as several species of fish and abundant waterfowl. A few people even swim in the lake, usually not until July and not for very long, for water temperatures are normally well below comfortable swimming levels. Children splash and wade along the lake's pebbly beaches, families hike the paved trails, and powerboaters churn the lake's surface with heavy horsepower. The lower lake has become a popular playground.

Even so, the lake still preserves the western shore, for few visitors venture beyond the shoreline vegetation. No question about it—the backcountry, especially where no trails lead in or out, can be dangerous: a moose might charge, defending its newborn calf, or a grizzly sow might attack, protecting its cubs. Every few years a visitor gets lost or falls from a cliff.

To avoid problems, follow park rules on the lake, on the roads, and in the backcountry. Speed limits—on the lake as well as on the roads—are designed to protect wildlife as well as park visitors. I once saw a mangled car and its injured passengers after a collision with a moose. The moose died—and for a few days attracted grizzly bears to the local dump. Fortunately, the people survived, but spent their vacation in the hospital.

Jackson Lake Lodge, completed in 1956, rests on a glacial moraine above the Willow Flats, which lie along the north shore of the lake's eastern arm near its outlet. The lodge with all its cabins, employee quarters, inappropriate swimming pool, corral, and gas station is situated on a hill in the heart of important wildlife habitat. Lodge guests have an opportunity to see many species of wildlife from grizzly bear (a jogger staying at the lodge was attacked the fall of 1995) to trumpeter swans (a pair usually nests on nearby Christian Pond). The huge picture windows of the lodge's great hall offer a view of the entire Teton Range that seems to rise from the waters of Jackson Lake where its majestic snow-clad peaks are reflected.

From the observation platform in front of the lodge, park visitors can watch moose browsing in the marsh between the lodge and the lakeshore, see beavers working in the shallow ponds at dusk, observe sandhill cranes dancing in the moist meadow and puddle ducks feeding in the beaver ponds.

In the spring of 1996 a young grizzly bear fed for several days in the Willow Flats between the lodge and the Snake River as it flows out of Jackson Lake at the dam. When tourists began to infringe upon its territory, the bear was livetrapped and removed, relocated into a wilderness area where it would be safe from tourist harassment.

For all the development that has occurred near the outlet of Jackson Lake and for all the tourist activity in the vicinity, the area still offers an amazing variety of wildlife, mountain vistas, wildflowers, and scenic splendor.

Buck-and-Pole Fences

The rustic fences so aesthetically pleasing to the eye and so often photographed by visitors to Jackson Hole are known as buck-and-pole fences because they are made of crossed timbers (bucks) and long stringers (poles) made of lodgepole pines. Given the glacial gravel and quartzite cobbles that compose the floor of the valley, postholes are all but impossible to dig: to dig a hole three feet deep, you end up with a depression six feet in diameter due to the angle of repose of the material you are digging into—it simply falls back into the hole and looks like a giant doodlebug (ant lion) den.

The abundant lodgepole pine serves as an ideal building material, and the bucks set on the surface obviate the need to dig postholes. Bison, moose, and winter snows break down fences made of lodgepole pine, but there are plenty more poles to be had on nearby national forest lands: with an inexpensive permit from the Forest Service, fencers can rebuild annually when it is necessary, but normally the fences function for years.

Buck-and-pole fences are common on the Jackson Hole valley floor. Postholes are too difficult to dig in the glacial outwash plain, and abundant poles are available in the nearby lodgepole pine forests. Photo by Verne Huser.

FEBRUARY 1999   PAUL HUBER

Section 3 (15 miles)

Jackson Lake Dam to Deadman's Bar

As the Snake River forms again after its impoundment in the reservoir, it flows clear and green, oxygenated—and probably nitrogenated too—by the plunge of surface water from the lake to the riverbed almost fifty feet below. Fishing and boating are prohibited for several hundred yards below the dam.

The fast water below the base of the dam, popular with pelicans and gulls, served as a rapid when *The Big Sky* was filmed on the Snake River in the mid-1950s. The keelboat *Mandan* used in the movie, tied to a huge eyebolt in the concrete base of the dam, seemed about to capsize and be swept away by the current in an exciting scene from the movie, based on the novel by Pulitzer Prize–winner A. B. Guthrie Jr. Guthrie also wrote the screenplay for *Shane,* a novel by Jack Schaefer that was also filmed in Jackson Hole in the 1950s.

The four- to five-mile segment immediately below the dam flows primarily with reservoir-release water. Spring Creek, Christian Creek, and local trickles from the adjacent beaver marsh on the left bank barely impact the cold, clear water released from the lake. Initially flowing east, the river hugs the base of Signal Mountain, then briefly bends away from the steep ridge, flowing northward toward Jackson Lake Lodge, which can be seen from the river, rising above Willow Flats. The flats are the large marshy area between Jackson Lake and a series of moraine hills to the north on which Jackson Lake Lodge and its array of cabins and other tourist accommodations reside.

Willow Flats is a great place to see moose, elk, and sandhill cranes; I saw the moose from Lunch Tree Hill the evening I met Margaret Altmann there. On the left bank a mile below the dam where the river swings sharply to the right to flow eastward again, the old Biological Research Station sponsored by the University of

A bull moose feeds in a small creek that drains Willow Flats into the Snake. Photo by Verne Huser.

Wyoming was once situated. This served as Margaret's home for the summer when she was not in the backcountry studying wildlife. There I heard many lectures and reports on wildlife studies going on in what is now called the Greater Yellowstone Ecosystem. (The station, now known as the University of Wyoming's Biological Research Center, has moved to the old AMK Ranch on Jackson Lake.)

Just over two miles from the dam lies Cattlemen's Bridge, a wooden structure designed to assist cattlemen who once grazed their livestock on public lands that have since been incorporated into the Grand Teton National Park. In recent years the bridge, which thankfully does not accommodate motorized traffic, was used primarily by fishermen and hikers, but flood damage and old age have closed it even to foot traffic. Park officials have contemplated removing it to protect the wild nature of the area to which it once provided access.

Within sight of Cattlemen's Bridge the Snake enters an oxbow, a large loop to the left that serves as a secondary river channel at high water but at low levels becomes a shallow backwater lake known as Oxbow Bend, one of the best wildlife-viewing areas in the park. I have seen otters, bear, elk, deer, moose, muskrats, beavers, trumpeter swans, bald eagles, osprey, white pelicans, great blue heron, Canada geese, several species of duck, and numerous other birds—all from my canoe on the Oxbow. The Bureau of Reclamation considered building a dam below the Oxbow—a dam that would have

In this view from Signal Mountain, Cattlemen's Bridge can be seen, spanning the Snake River. The Oxbow loops to the left. Photo by Verne Huser.

inundated the greatest wildlife habitat in the park. Unbelievably, this was one of the options studied in 1984 when the bureau completed its Environmental Impact Statement for the mid-1980s repair of Jackson Lake Dam.

Dams and Dikes

Because the valley floor tilts to the west, the town of Wilson at the foot of Teton Pass is lower than the Snake River. In order to protect private property, the U.S. Army Corps of Engineers has for decades tried to keep the river from flowing downhill, from finding its way to the lowest levels of the valley floor along the fault. It has not worked too well, and it has been an expensive proposition, both financially and in habitat loss.

Large, expensive homes have become a common sight in the Snake River floodplain. In high-water years, a flood sweeps down the valley, threatening multimillion-dollar homes and estates. Home owners, in turn, threaten the county, which permitted them to build where they did, with lawsuits. The dikes and levees are shorn up at public expense to protect private properties that should never have been considered viable building sites.

Neither are dams a satisfactory answer, permanently flooding miles of valuable riparian habitat and sometimes creating floods somewhere else,

Homes such as this one, built in the Snake River floodplain, are at great peril in high-water years. Photo by Verne Huser.

at some other time. Dams and dikes disturb natural patterns and make the riverine environment ugly. In response to environmental concerns, the U.S. Army Corps of Engineers is making restoration studies. At this time, however, the Corps is expected only to create some backwaters.

There is a seeming lunacy to this futile and costly pattern of "natural" disasters. If you build in the floodplain, you are eventually going to be flooded. Rivers need a place to go, and when restricted by dikes and levees, they are bound to flood somewhere else.

U.S. Highway 89/191/287 runs north of the Oxbow and immediately adjacent to it, offering one of the more popular scenic turnouts in the park. A gravel road leading to Cattlemen's Bridge turns off the highway just west of the Oxbow, offering access to the Oxbow in an ideal canoe launch site near the bridge, a gradually sloping shoreline in slow-moving water.

The large meadow northeast of the Oxbow once served as a bison and elk pasture during the late 1950s and early 1960s, part of a "wildlife park" where native species were confined; before that, the fenced bison pasture lay west of the Oxbow. Bison and elk now roam freely, having escaped often enough to frustrate the Park Service in its attempts to recapture them. It also reflects a more humane and ecologically sound wildlife management philosophy.

Prior to the 1960s bison and elk browsed together at the old Wildlife Exhibition Pasture on the Oxbow of the Snake River. Photo by Verne Huser.

The two-mile stretch from the Oxbow to the mouth of Pacific Creek flows fast, deep, and clear through important elk calving ground in spring, good bear habitat in summer and fall, and a major elk crossing during spring and fall migrations. This short section of river abounds in beavers as well; a large lodge has for many years dominated the lower point between the Snake and its oxbow. An evening paddle there will surely provide canoeists with several encounters with beavers looking for breakfast, for they normally spend daylight hours in their lodges, emerging at dusk to break their daylong fast.

A historic boat access known as Pacific Creek Landing is found on the left bank between the mouths of Pacific Creek and Buffalo Fork. During the filming of *The Big Sky*, the movie crew cut down the steep bank to facilitate launching the keelboat *Mandan* used in the film. That launch site served the Grand Teton Lodge Company's float trip operation for several years (1956-1960) until the National Park Service established the present river access upstream and eventually paved it. The Mandan Cut lies about fifty yards downstream from the present paved access. A pair of kingfishers once nested in the cut bank on the left between the modern and historic launch sites.

Buffalo Fork enters the Snake from the left as the river swings south and begins to braid and meander into the Buffalo Channels. For the next mile extensive silt from the Buffalo's agricultural valley enters the Snake and alters its flow. Always muddy during the spring snowmelt runoff, the Buffalo adds color and nutrients—massive amounts of silt, sand, and suspended materials—to the clear reservoir-release waters of the Snake. Beaver dams have created extensive marshes that mark the confluence with abundant beaver sign; because of these dams, the confluence area often appears flooded even after high waters recede. Several large lodges have existed in this vicinity in recent decades.

At this point the river has changed massively during the more than forty years I have floated it. Spring floods have cut new channels, abandoned old ones, and deposited silt and gravel beds and bars, undercut forested banks, and generally altered the course of this stretch of the Snake. Spruce Ditch—a narrow, deep, swift-flowing channel cut by the Snake in the late 1950s—no longer exists. A leaning spruce tree, undercut by high water, fell across the channel one night in early June 1959. It caused a minor problem for the Lodge Company pontoon the next morning—passengers had to walk the log to shore before boatmen Frank Ewing and I extracted the pontoon, then reloaded the passengers and continued our trip—but that evening it very nearly ended a child's life and created a family tragedy.

Park ranger Dunbar Susong and his family, including an infant daughter, floated the Snake late that same afternoon. Unaware of the fallen tree, Dunbar took the Spruce Ditch channel, which he had used many times before. When their small raft hit the fallen tree, the flimsy inflatable swept beneath the log, and dumped everyone into the river. Trapped underwater, the eighteen-month-old child nearly drowned before her father freed her; only her father's mouth-to-mouth resuscitation, a technique that had just come into use at the time, saved her life. However, the family, soaking wet and cold and stranded on the wrong side of the river, had to walk miles to safety, using Cattlemen's Bridge to cross the river.

No one died that night, but Dunbar's heroic self-rescue effort taught a generation of Snake River boaters an important lesson: be prepared for anything and everything, and never underestimate the river. Lodge Company boatmen, at the Park Service's request, removed the fallen tree the following day (current Park Service policy allows only rare removal of natural hazards). Over the years, Spruce Ditch first widened, then silted in, and finally disappeared as its forming banks washed away, but for a generation of guides who knew about the accident, Spruce Ditch remains a vital part of Snake River lore.

The lower end of the braided area serves as a major elk crossing. One spring Frank Ewing and I observed a herd of about eighty cows and calves fording there, and summering elk often hang out in the meadow on the left bank even today, an area early boatmen named the Elk Meadow. The aspen-covered ridge to the right (Aspen Ridge) offers cover for elk about to cross, and the fringe of timber on the left also gives them visual protection and cover.

The heavily timbered right bank below the elk crossing, sometimes called the Otter Bank by early boatmen, was once home to a family of otters. Walt Disney's film crew photographed the otter family there in the 1950s, giving the area the name Disney Bank. The river bends to the right below Disney Bank as it approaches Spring Bank Bend on the left, an area where irrigated hayfields bleed water back into the Snake.

On the inside of the curve at Spring Bank Bend lies a gravel bar at lower water levels, a favorite coyote bathing beach. In the early days of Snake River boating we frequently found coyotes sunning themselves on this bar to dry off after bathing in the shallow water on the inside of the bend. The left bank at the lower end of the curve becomes Bank Swallow Bend for the numerous birds that nested there, digging tunnels into the bank, laying their eggs at the end of the tunnels, and raising their young only a few inches from the river. In high-water years, many swallow nests flood or wash away. Below the Bank Swallow Bend the high-water overflow stream known as the Disney Channel reenters the Snake on the right as the river bends left.

At this bend a spectacular view of the Teton Range appears downstream, a scenic turnout on the river, so to speak. As the peaks come into view, the river begins a straight run for more than a mile. Near the end of that mile Spread Creek enters on the left across from the RKO Landing, an old river access point and the location of film crew camps for such movies as *The Big Sky*. One summer a great horned owl raised a brood of four owlets near the mouth of Spread Creek; for nearly a month float trip passengers could see all four of the fluffy young birds every morning on an arched snag in the middle of the creek.

At this point too we often watched battles between osprey and red-tailed hawks. Once we watched an osprey catch a trout and fly with it toward a nearby nest. When an eagle attacked from above, hoping to steal the trout, the osprey dropped the fish and turned upside down to defend itself. The eagle abandoned the battle and swooped down to catch the falling fish in midair and fly away with a free meal.

Below Spread Creek the river enters a broad S-curve with an island or two splitting small channels off the main river at the bends in an ever changing pattern. The islands come and go as the river eats into the bank and alters its course. Here the low sagebrush flats on the right bank give way to heavy timber, the site of an old eagle's nest and a gold-mining operation, both long since abandoned. We used to be able to spot the adult eagles from a half-mile away, perched on an open branch of the lone blue spruce on the left bank. This bank, composed of eroded glacial outwash, is much higher than the one at Bank Swallow Bend and serves as home for another bank swallow colony, the high-rise district. Here, attracted by the sound of cascading gravel, I once saw a badger digging into the colony to feed on swallow eggs and hatchlings.

The gold-mining operation on the west bank, directly across the river from the Swallow Bank, served as an excuse for two old bachelors to camp on the Snake several summers in the 1950s until the Park Service challenged their gold-mining claims and, through legal action, removed them from the park. The glacial gravels of Jackson Hole contain several billion dollars' worth of flour gold so fine that it has never paid to mine it—even in the early days of gold fever throughout the West or the $800-per-ounce gold prices of the early 1980s.

A half mile below the gold diggings, we once saw a black bear feeding on the carcass of a beaver. The area became the BBBC Bend (Bear By Beaver Carcass) to a handful of boatmen, but the name never really stuck. Mountain bluebirds nest in the small aspen grove on the left bank, and both pronghorn and bison enjoy the neighborhood west of the river, crossing frequently through the shallow waters of the next mile or two in their quest for varied grazing.

At a sharp bend of the river to the left lies a group of small islands that guides collectively named Bull Moose Island for the lone bull moose that frequented that particular clump of islands. In 1993 when Roderick Nash, Frank Ewing, and I floated the Snake on a nostalgia trip—we had all run the Snake together the summer of 1957—I decided to test my companions' memories. "What's the name of that island?" I asked.

"I believe that's Bull Moose Island," said Frank.

"Yeah, and there's one right now," Rod added.

Looking downstream, we saw a large, dark animal. "Its tail's too long for a moose," I said. That is when we all realized at once that we were observing a small herd of bison: bulls, cows, and calves, some on the right bank, some on the islands, some in the water through which we floated gingerly within a few yards of several of the shaggy beasts.

Around this island-marked bend where ravens sometimes congregate on the left bank, the river begins to split up: one channel goes left toward the Triangle X Ranch (Triangle X Channel), which floaters can see from there; the main channel continues relatively straight for another mile. Then the whole river splits apart into several channels that weave and part, rejoin and split again for the next two or three miles. Guides call this section the Spread. A pair of bald eagles nested in the Spread a few years ago, but due to channel changes they later abandoned the nest. The Spread attracts pronghorn and coyotes and offers fine views of the Tetons.

However, one of the best views of the Tetons comes as the numerous channels reunite to cut a gorge through the glacial moraine in the Snake's deepest segment within the park. High glacial-debris ridges close in from both sides as the river turns west toward the range, offering a well-framed view downriver. A few midstream rocks produce a mild rapid and require a little maneuvering, but the sounds of moving water bouncing off the steep banks add to the thrill and the sense of adventure.

When then-secretary of the interior Stewart Udall and his family floated the river with me in 1961, a congregation of ravens dotted the steep cut bank on the left at the entrance to the gorge. We were into naming river features that day, and Udall suggested Raven Ridge as an appropriate name for the bank—and so it is known today, at least in the minds of several early river guides.

The mountains disappear behind the steep edge of the outwash plain as the river approaches the Burned Ridge moraine and the modern access point known as Deadman's Bar. Both bald and golden eagles often sit on this steep bank or soar along its edge to catch updrafts. On rare but special occasions bison graze on the lip of the ridge, silhouetted against the skyline—one of my favorite sights.

I am convinced the historic Deadman's Bar lies on the right bank, not on the left, and above the bend. I explored the area on foot before the Park Service closed it and found the old sluice canals. Prickly pear cacti grow uncharacteristically on the bench above. My hunch is supported by the account written in 1929 by ranger Fritiof Fryxell for the *Annals of Wyoming*. What is now called Deadman's Bar lies south and east, not north of the river. The official Bridger-Teton National Forest map for the Buffalo and Jackson Ranger Districts, which includes Grand Teton National Park, has it marked correctly, however.

On the inside of the bend lies the modern access, crowded much of the summer because this is where most commercial river outfitters launch their float trips. The Grand Teton Lodge Company's small-boat trips stop here to exchange passengers, but their baloney boats (pontoons) round the bend to stop on the left bank at their meal site. Many fishermen initiate their guided trips here too. It is one of the busiest sites on the whole river.

Section 4 (10.5 miles)

Deadman's Bar to Moose Village

Deadman's Bar may sound ominous, but it is really a welcoming place, a river access with a fringe of forest growing along the east bank: narrow-leafed cottonwoods and blue spruce, the most common climax species along the river. In the parking area farther from the river a few broadleaf cottonwoods grow, readily distinguishable from the narrow-leafed variety by their larger leaves. It is the bark of these broadleaf trees that the mountain men used to feed their horses during the deep snows of winter, a practice they learned from Native Americans. The Indians knew better than to winter in Jackson Hole; they nonetheless knew how to keep their horses alive during winter conditions.

When I launch at Deadman's Bar, I point out two features of the immediate landscape that serve as teaching tools: the river's movement over midstream rocks that creates the only section of rapids, mild though they are, in this segment of the Snake; and the angle of repose of the opposite bank, which rises almost two hundred feet above the river and blocks out the view of the Teton peaks. *Angle of repose* is the term used to denote the maximum degree of grade that a slope can have and still be "at rest." Beyond the angle of repose, gravity will cause a hillside to slide or its components to roll downslope. I ask my passengers to note the high banks that confine the river here. The high terrace across the river from our launch site as well as upstream approaches forty-five degrees, a fairly standard slope (angle of repose) found throughout the valley.

As we move into the current, I usually row to midstream through the rocks so that my passengers can observe a simple pattern: on the river the water moves but the waves stand still, created by underwater obstacles that remain stationary. On a lake or in the ocean, however, the waves move, but the water remains still, any given molecule of water merely bobbing up and down as waves pass through.

When my passengers look downstream here, they see that the

Deadman's Bar lies below the Snake River Overlook on U.S. Highway 26/89/187 east of the Snake River in Grand Teton National Park. It is the site of a major launch area (off to the right in this view) and the Grand Teton Lodge Company's meal site, which offers an impressive view of the Teton Range across the river. Photo by Verne Huser.

angle of repose increases, approaching the vertical. We drift toward the moraine dam on the west left by the last major valley glacier, the Burned Ridge moraine, which once formed a glacial lake at this point. There the glacier, as it started to melt back, dumped its massive load of rock debris, receding in the warming climate of post-glacial times. Such rock debris contains every size of material: huge boulders, coarse and small gravel, even sand and fine silt. Known as glacial till, it is a mixture that holds moisture and can consequently

The angle of repose is evident at the edge of the glacial outwash above Deadman's Bar. Photo by Verne Huser.

support trees and vegetation. It also holds together at steeper angles of repose than glacial outwash.

As we drift through the moraine's natural dam, we can see a layer of clay in the right bank. This clay layer, which was first exposed during the flood of 1996, is composed of fine silt and glacial flour. Impervious to water, it marks the bottom of an ancient glacial lake, the dam that created it having been cut through by an earlier and much larger Snake River. The valley floor is filled to a depth of several thousand feet with glacial debris, but the turbulent river that resulted from the melting of the glacial ice washed away the fine materials, leaving a level plain devoid of enough soil to hold the moisture necessary for tree growth near the surface of the plain. Thus, a broad, flat valley with few trees results: though there is plenty of water, there simply is not enough soil to hold moisture near enough to the surface to support tree life.

The low terrace on the left just before the river bends to the right is the Grand Teton Lodge Company's meal site—has been for years—where their float trip passengers stop for breakfast, lunch, or dinner.

In this view from Blacktail Butte, Cottonwood Creek enters the Snake to the left of center, following the funnel-shaped valley filled with cottonwood trees. Ditch Creek enters the river proper in foreground. The mountains, left to right, are Grand Teton, Mount Owen, and Teewinot; the Saint John's Group (serrated); and Mount Moran. Timber Island appears at far right below Mount Moran. Photo by Verne Huser.

Glimpses of the Teton Peaks

Not only faith but also your perspective from the river can move mountains. From the northeast part of the valley near the mouth of the Buffalo Fork, Mount Moran appears the largest peak in the range. In late summer its black dike stands out prominently, and its sedimentary cap appears from beneath the melting snow. The Cathedral Group—Grand Teton, Mount Owen, and Teewinot—disappears into insignificance, blending into the mass of the range as specific canyons mark various peaks.

However, as you drift southwest down the Snake, this latter trio of major peaks becomes more prominent: Teewinot on the left, the Grand in the middle, and Mount Owen to the right—all south of Cascade Canyon, which bisects the range. At one point you can see Table Mountain on the west slope as you look up Cascade Canyon. From the vicin-

The Teton Glacier lies beneath the north face of Grand Teton. Gunsight Notch appears at the right. Photo by Verne Huser.

ity of Deadman's Bar—both upstream and downstream (but not at the bar itself, for it lies in the deepest part of the outwash plain)—Mount Owen disappears altogether behind Teewinot, and the Grand towers above them all. Downstream Mount Owen emerges again between the summit of the Grand and Teewinot at the head of Glacier Gulch where the Teton Glacier lies. As you drift down the river, the peaks continue to change position in relation to your position on the river: you see the whole panorama.

Teton Glacier

Glaciers are rivers of ice that flow slowly down the canyons, carving their sides, gouging out rocks, and both pushing debris before them and carrying debris on their broad, icy backs. The Teton Glacier lies in the hollow between Grand Teton and Teewinot below Gunsight Notch and can be seen from the river from several points below the Old Eagle Nest.

The Grand Teton, tallest peak in the range and from this point on the river obviously so, tops a ridge that joins it to Mount Owen. A sharp declivity, Gunsight Notch, marks the low point on this ridge. The Teton Glacier begins immediately below this notch. It flows roughly two-thirds of a mile to its terminal moraine in Glacier Gulch, which can be seen as a dam of gray rock debris at the lower aspect of the canyon. More than one thousand feet wide, it is reported to be several hundred feet deep and flows at a rate of about twenty-five meters per year.

As you approach the bend where Grand Teton Lodge Company passengers take their meals, notice the two point bars, both on inside bends: one upstream on the left above the Lodge Company landing, the other on the right as the river bends to the right. At high water the right-hand bar becomes an island; at very high water—flood stage—it disappears, and the river overflows the right bank, taking a shortcut to the channel below the bend, leaving behind a new layer of silt on the low river bench.

We round the bend, and passengers have their first view of the Tetons from the river, towering above the edge of the outwash plain, a matchless photo opportunity. The high bank to the left, part of the terminal moraine, exhibits the greatest variety of trees growing anywhere along the river: Douglas fir (not a true fir), subalpine fir (many of them dead or dying), blue spruce, limber pine (high on the ridge), a scattering of lodgepole pines, a few ancient cottonwoods, and an occasional aspen. This well-watered bank has a huge snow cornice in the late winter and early spring that often lasts into July. When fishing season opened each year on April 1, veteran river runner and fisherman Charlie Sands used to slide his inflatable raft down this snow chute to get on the river to fish where no one else would compete.

At the bend a huge boulder, known as Boy Scout Rock, lies near midriver. At high water it creates a powerful hydraulic; at more moderate water levels, a beckoning bit of whitewater for young canoeists. The rock, which stands high out of the water at low river levels, carries numerous colorful scars from contact with Boy Scout—and other—canoe bottoms. The Scouts no longer canoe this stretch of the Snake; they use paddle rafts instead, a safer means of adventure transportation.

Another rapid appears near the left bank at the base of a clay cliff that first appeared during the summer of 1996, the flood year that exposed the old glacial lake bottom upstream—perhaps this is part of the same layer. Created by huge blocks of rough-surfaced rocks, this rapid should be avoided by raft or canoe. It represents evidence of ancient volcanism in the Yellowstone area. Known to geologists as a welded tuff, this material resulted from a *nuee ardente,* or fiery breath, a blast of hot gases and molten rock that came from miles away in one of the numerous pyroclastic events that mark the geologic history of Yellowstone. It has left a layer of porous rock with a rough surface, the result of hot gases escaping from the molten material as it began to cool and harden. A layer of this material exists on the left bank, but several large, rough boulders have fallen into the Snake, creating a bit of whitewater near the steep left bank.

The river flows toward the mountains for nearly a mile in one of its longest straight stretches, approaching the high cut bank on the right. Bald eagles often perch in the tall blue spruce along the left bank, and we have frequently seen bear in this vicinity. At low water a gravel island appears in midriver. As the river bends left at the lower end of the island, a few large rocks create waves near the right bank. It is best to avoid them unless you want to get wet.

The river bends left, growing shallow and creating a natural ford or crossing used especially by bison and pronghorn. Migrating elk have scarred the steep-cut bank on the right with trails leading to summer pastures in Yellowstone; in early summer tall blue penstemon bloom there, attracting hummingbirds. Several rocks from the welded tuff, carried by high water to this bend, mark the inside of the curve and serve as resting sites for sunning American mergansers, a common duck along the river. Below this cut bank, a narrow fringe of blue spruce trees marks the right shore, a nesting area for ravens and a nocturnal drinking spot for elk migrating down to

The notorious Bump Stump with an ill-fated pontoon wrapped around it.
Photo by Verne Huser.

the river at night from the conifer forest on the Burned Ridge moraine. We have seen bear in this forest fringe that offers a screen from river traffic.

At the lower end of the timber fringe on the right, a few old cottonwoods show scars from beaver work; I suspect a den lies under the bank near a tiny spring that trickles into the Snake. The left-bank vegetation shows evidence of extensive beaver work, and the lower right bank, with its willows and young cottonwoods, provides one of the best places to see beavers at dusk.

The Bump Stump was named in 1959 for a dude ranch's pontoon raft that hit into this snag in midriver and remained wrapped around it for several days. Anchored to the river bottom, that snag reminds river runners of hazards and changes. Now located near an island well to the right, the snag has not moved, but the river has. In the late 1950s the Bump Stump lay so near the left bank it was difficult to steer a course to the left of it. The Snake has cut away at least 150 feet of that heavily forested riverbank on the left and deposited a long, shallow island near midstream that threatens to join the right bank.

Below the Bump Stump the river has made its greatest changes during recent flood years, building as much as two hundred feet on the left bank and cutting away an equal amount of the right, all but obliterating the Forest Channels. Numerous tall spruce and cottonwoods have fallen into the Snake, but other trees have become more available to beavers. An ancient beaver lodge on the right bank washed away in the 1996 flood, but that same flood cut away so much bank that trees too far from the river to attract beavers before the flooding suddenly became available delicacies.

The Snake begins serious meandering and dividing at this point, some three miles below Deadman's Bar. The floods of 1996 and 1997 have rearranged the river there, creating new channels and obliterating old ones. A family of otters used to live in this vicinity, and a pair of mountain bluebirds has nested there in recent years. The only patch of a lovely wildflower known as river beauty in Alaska, but locally called willow weed, bloomed there, but the floods have no doubt scoured it away—as they have the pink monkey flowers that grew along the right bank near the Bar B C Ranch downstream. The good news is that the floods have also scoured the yellow-blossomed sweet clover, which is an invasive alien, off the river bars.

With the old Forest Channels inaccessible and the route into Line Camp closed, the right side of the river at this point has been temporarily lost to floaters (but not to wildlife) along with the channel that flows past Otter Bank, but it will return when another flood year rearranges the river. Massive piles of dead trees have blocked a number of old channels, creating wildlife habitat and allowing the right side of the river to recover from overfishing and from float trip traffic. Bison often frequent this area, especially the right bank, but one old solitary bull likes the left bank, an area formerly known as Upper Schwabacher.

Beaver activity in the next mile or two has increased since the flood years. Beaver families whose lodges were washed away by the high water have regrouped to cut numerous trees and build new lodges. In the summer of 1996, beginning almost as soon as the waters began to recede, beavers cut more than twenty-five trees on the left bank in a matter of six weeks. Normally, the tree cutting does not begin until fall, but because the river had wrecked their old

The Gros Ventre slide created a natural dam that washed out in 1927. The devastation caused by the resulting flash flood is evident here.
Courtesy of U.S. Forest Service.

habitat, they got an early start and built an enormous new lodge on an island near the old line camp cabin just above the Otter Bank.

Although a few channels trickle through to the left, the main channel swings against the right-hand shore as the lower end of Otter Bank gives way to Peekaboo Bend. When the new channel (Peekaboo Street) opened in 1996, a lone cottonwood tree stood sentinel at the entrance, but the high water was eating away at its roots. We decided that as long as the tree stood, it was safe to use the channel, but if it disappeared, it had probably gone down the Street and might block the channel.

Colette, one of the Barker-Ewing guides, had never tried Peekaboo Street, but at high-water levels, it proved the safest route on the river. I volunteered to lead her down it for her first run, suggesting that she follow my boat by about a hundred yards. As I approached the opening of the channel, the tree still stood, but its top seemed agitated. I entered the channel with no trouble, but when we were sixty yards into it, one of my passengers yelled "Look!" and pointed upstream. Just as Colette's boat entered the channel, the cottonwood began to topple. It missed her boat by only a few feet, scaring the wits out of me.

I shouted at Colette, pointing upstream, but she could not read my signs or hear me. She wondered what she had done wrong. She never did see the tree fall until it was in the river, tearing loose from the bank and floating down behind her. It missed the opening to the channel we had taken and ended up on a brush pile in the main channel that was already blocked. Colette was nowhere near as frightened by the experience as I was.

The Gros Ventre Slide

From the west side of the river as the Snake swings left at Peekaboo Bend, floaters can see the scar left by the Gros Ventre slide. In 1925 50 million cubic yards of rocks, earth, and forest slid off the north end of Sheep Mountain into the valley of the Gros Ventre River, a major Snake River tributary in Jackson Hole. The massive landslide, witnessed by a horseman who outrode its rockfall but felt the sudden wind generated by the slide, spooned several hundred feet up the north (opposite) side of the valley and dammed the river, forming a large lake. In 1927 that lake breached the natural dam in a tremendous flash flood that wiped out the town of Kelly, drowned six people, inundated the entire Snake River Valley downstream, and caused flood damage all the way to the Idaho border. A drive to see the slide and its remaining lake takes only an hour and is well worth the time—and you might even see bighorn sheep.

The river has changed massively in the stretch below the old eagle's nest: old channels gone, new ones formed overnight, then blocked the next day, main channels relegated to minor ones, banks washed away, and *hundreds* of trees in the river, new snags every day. One day the right side of the river would be blocked; the next day it would be the left. We keep a chalkboard in the boathouse to mark open and closed channels; it changed hourly during the high water.

The left channel, when it is open, goes to Lower Schwabacher Landing; the right could go through Dead End Right and into the Maze or, following the old main channel, through Klog's Escape or Smiley's Slip to a confluence with Schwabacher Channel and on to Spruce Divide. In any case a herd of elk summers in this maze of islands that some call the Big Island, usually well protected by shallow channels and heavy timber. At high water many of the old channels, like my favorite, Bar B C, may be open, providing access to some excellent wildlife viewing.

The Wall

From the Snake River in the vicinity of Schwabacher Channel on the east side of the river, floaters can see a dark limestone formation known as the Wall at the head of Avalanche Canyon that represents the sedimentary layers that once covered the entire Teton Range. These ancient beds have been eroded away from the east face of the range except for the remnant on the summit of Mount Moran and this five-hundred-foot vertical wall marking the upper reach of the southern-most canyon in the high peaks area. An old trail, long since abandoned because of excessive rockfall, once crossed the Wall, which can be reached by a long hike up the South Fork of Cascade Canyon and over the divide between the South Teton and the Wall—or by a bushwhack up the trailless Avalanche Canyon. The view is worth the steep hike.

The complex of channels and islands from the old Eagle's Nest to the head of Many Moose Island—four to five miles, depending on which channels you take—offers the best wildlife on this stretch of river, but it remains the most challenging. A number of drownings on private trips, numerous canoe accidents, and at least one kayak fatality have occurred in this vicinity. Undercut by the high-water current, two trees have fallen across commercial rafts, leading to one fatality and several injuries. One commercial raft hit a trio of overhanging trees just below Spruce Divide in the summer of 1996, capsizing and dumping its passengers and guide into the cold, swift water. This section of river should be taken seriously.

The right side of the river—Deadend and its various outlet channels—became known as the Maze for its intricate network of small, fast channels. One year the Maze closed completely, but three outlets—Door One, Door Two, and Door Three—let boats through until one after the other they were blocked. Then the maze (Door Four) blew open and began wearing away at both banks: from a width of only fifty feet in 1995, it widened to more than two hundred by 1998, depositing several nasty snags to make floating more danger-

The Wall as seen from the outlet of Snowdrift Lake.
Photo by Verne Huser.

ous and difficult but also creating new islands where waterfowl can nest and moose can safely have their calves.

The Snake, dammed as it is at the outlet of the natural Jackson Lake, experiences delayed flood levels. The reservoir capacity added by the forty-foot dam creates an unnatural flow regime that not only alters the natural condition of the river but also interferes with natural reproduction patterns of the waterfowl species that depend on the river for appropriate nesting conditions.

The river comes back together briefly below the Bar B C Ranch on the right bank. Depending upon which channel you float, you either drift right by the ranch or see it back upstream on the opposite channel. Since 1996 the river essentially flows in one channel for the next mile because the entrance to Many Moose Right has become blocked. This channel, shallow and fairly narrow, offered one of the best wildflower and wildlife channels on the river, everything from elephantheads, fringed gentian, grass of Parnassas, and yellow monkey flowers to bald eagles fishing, baby beavers testing their skills, mule deer feeding, sandhill cranes nesting, and a big bull bison just hanging out.

Below Bar B C the river flows toward a favorite eagle perch in a massive cottonwood on the left bank. The female of this pair of eagles, whose nest lies a quarter mile up Cottonwood Creek, has an uncharacteristic white spot on her breast. The river then bends right to bombard Many Moose Island, which the river flooded in both 1996 and 1997, threatening to open a new channel right through the island. Beavers dominated this bank in the summer of 1996 as they began cutting several trees by midsummer.

The river swings back to the left; it opened a new channel—or, rather, created a new access to an old channel—in the summer of 1997. We thought it might cut through in 1996, but the entrance remained blocked all summer. However, in 1997 it blew out, and as long as the water remained high, we could again float the old Rookery Channel that has been closed for decades.

Just below this new entrance, the river went crazy in 1996 and again in 1997 as channels opened and closed on a daily basis, the river choking on trees washed downstream, being blocked briefly, then blowing out new routes through the network of snags during high water, resulting in our losing the Teton Marsh Channel and the lower left-hand side of the river—temporarily. There are changes every year somewhere along the way.

Last Chance Channel opened briefly during 1996, then closed again as water levels dropped. Floods change the river, change the behavior of its wildlife and the location of its wildflowers. In any area where the river braids, count on its altering its course every few years, especially during record high-water years, and be alert for new obstacles, for current differences.

Even the mouth of Cottonwood Creek, which drains Jenny Lake

into the Snake, has changed in recent years: it once flowed into the river from the north, then from the west. Recently, it turned to the north, flowing into the Snake from the south. Over the years the creek created a broad delta and now spreads out to enter the Snake in a series of small, cold clear-water channels. Along this delta yellow monkey flowers and pale-blue forget-me-nots bloom for much of the summer, and you can often see one or the other of the eagles perched on a dead limb, perhaps even one of the recently fledged eaglets.

Below the mouth of Cottonwood Creek, the river finally comes back together for its last mile. It bends right around the 4 Lazy F Ranch at a corner where a small grove of limber pines grows on the river's edge; one giant leaning upstream at a forty-five-degree angle finally succumbed and fell into the river in 1999.

A colony of coal-black marmots once lived along the right shore immediately below the 4 Lazy F Corner, but I have not seen one in years. Today on the right bank you may find one or two of the big bull moose lying in the shade on hot afternoons or a quartet of mule deer bucks feeding at dusk—they sometimes appear in the parking lot at Moose Landing.

Ditch Creek, which flows through the Teton Science School, enters from the east (left) across from the 4 Lazy F. Raccoons like the vicinity, great horned owls have nested there, and both bald eagles and osprey occasionally fish from the tall dead trees on the left bank, which grows a colorful patch of wildflowers throughout the summer. Chokecherry and silverberry, red osier dogwood and serviceberry all grow along the right bank, both above and below Menor's Ferry, a replica of which still runs across the Snake at its original site a quarter mile above Moose Landing.

Dornan's Moose Enterprise lines the left bank with cabins as well as a bar, deli, grocery store, gift shop, chuck-wagon restaurant, a pair of tall tipis, and the best wine cellar in Wyoming. If you look carefully as you drift downstream between Menor's Ferry and the landing, you can find the location of the 1927 bridge that put the ferry out of business. It is worth a side trip to explore the historical site on the right bank where Maud Noble's cabin and the Chapel of the Transfiguration still stand. If you visit at the right time, you might even have a chance to ride the ferry across the river. You are back in civilization at Moose Landing. Visit the museum and bookshop at park headquarters to learn more about the Snake and the rest of Jackson Hole.

PAUL M. HASER   FEBRUARY 1999

Section 5 (32 miles)

Moose Village to South Park

From the river access at Moose, site of Grand Teton National Park Headquarters, the Snake flows beneath a concrete bridge built in 1957. Bridge pilings offer a man-made hazard for river runners to avoid. I saw a Boy Scout die when the river's powerful current folded the canoe in which he was a passenger around the western piling. No one could reach him or save him. I have never felt so helpless in my life. People die almost every year on the Snake because they fail to realize its great potential for creating disastrous and unexpected circumstances when boaters do not know how to handle a boat, do not understand the basic rules of river hydraulics, and do not recognize the power of the river, the force of its current.

Moose feed along the Snake in this vicinity, often causing major traffic jams during the height of the tourist season. Tourists stop their cars in the middle of the bridge, foolishly blocking traffic so that someone can get a look at one of the big bulls that loiter there. A group of large buck mule deer often hangs out near the bridge; I have also seen a bear swim the river at this point.

Below the bridge the Snake bends gently to the west, then begins to braid and meander again. The Murie Ranch lies on the right bank around this bend. Olaus and Mardy, Ade and Weezy Murie bought the old STS Ranch in the mid-1940s. Eventually, the cabins on the property became summer dwellings for family and friends as well as for numerous guests, mostly members of the greater conservation community. Many major decisions in the ongoing battle to save wilderness and wildlife species have been made at this historic ranch, which will ultimately become an environmental research and education center, an environmental think tank associated with the Teton Science School.

To the west Snake River water trickles out of the river through the glacial gravels to form numerous backwaters and ponds, many of them enhanced by beaver activity. Keeping in mind that the valley floor of Jackson Hole tilts to the west and that the lowest part of the valley lies at the base of the range, you can understand the proclivity of the water to flow westward. The area between the Snake River and Sawmill Ponds on the Moose-Wilson Road, occupied largely by the Murie Ranch, constitutes a major natural wildlife sanctuary where deer, elk and moose, many rodents (beavers, muskrats, porcupines, red squirrels, northern flying squirrels) and members of the weasel family (weasels, marten, mink, skunks), and great gray owls thrive in a largely unvisited wetland created by the Snake River.

The first building of the Teton Science School is found on the left along the Moose-Wilson Road a few miles southwest of the Murie Ranch, near the turnoff (right) to Whitegrass Ranch and Phelps Lake.

There are only two short miles—from the mouth of Ditch Creek to the end of the first bend below the Moose Bridge—in which the Snake flows in a single channel, a fact that Bill Menor observed in 1894 when he selected the site for his ferry. The river's braiding and meandering continues below the Murie Ranch all the way to the Wilson Bridge and beyond, despite the U.S. Army Corps of Engineers' dikes and levees that begin at the park boundary. These dikes are now scheduled to be removed.

The Majors and the Teton Science School

Ted and Joan Major founded the Teton Science School the summer of 1967, the year I started guiding the partnership boat for Barker-Ewing Scenic Float Trips. We took the first class down the Snake River, starting a tradition that continues today. Teton Science School students have always been among our favorite passengers.

A year after graduating from Utah State University, where he studied science education, Ted Major along with his wife moved to Wyoming to accept a position teaching science in Jackson Hole under Superintendent Jerry Wimberley. Wimberley, who gave his full support to—and high school credit for—a summer field biology program, let Ted use the school facilities, an old bus, and the school library. Thus, the Teton Science School began as a day school for a six-week summer course in high school biology.

The second summer the school operated out of tents in Soldier Meadow near the Flagg Ranch section of the Snake in what is now the John D. Rockefeller Jr. Memorial Parkway, students and faculty camping

The Teton Science School compound, founded in 1967 by Ted and Joan Major, nestles on Ditch Creek. Courtesy of Jackie Gilmore.

on Polecat Creek for eight weeks with a special-use permit from the Forest Service. Geologist David Love, who supported the school, discovered high levels of radon gas in the vicinity at nearby Huckleberry Hot Springs, and the commercial pool was soon closed and buried. I began teaching with Ted at Jackson High School the following fall.

Board members of the fledgling school—John and Georgie Morgan, Virginia Huidekoper, artist Grant (Tiny) Hagen, and Elaine DuPont Jones—all gave their full support, as did Grand Teton National Park superintendent Howard Chapman. By the summer of 1969 the school had moved into the old Haines cabin on the Moose-Wilson Road in the park near the Murie Ranch. That summer Mardy Murie got involved and has been involved ever since.

In 1973 the Majors' dream became a year-round school and moved to its present quarters on Ditch Creek. There the stream flows out of the hills to the east of Jackson Hole behind Blacktail Butte, away from most tourist traffic, and at the eastern edge of Antelope Flats where bison browse, elk graze, and moose munch the willows. Major fund-raising activities and massive support from Grand Teton National Park helped the school expand. Dick Barker, Patty Ewing, and my former wife, Jean Jorgenson, have all served on the school's board.

The school soon began offering middle school and elementary school short courses during the school year—students came from several states—and, during summers, high school field ecology courses. An adult education program began, offering visiting lecturers, college

Ted Major lectures students of the Teton Science School. Photo by Verne Huser.

courses, teacher workshops, and Elderhostel opportunities during summers and in the "off-season"—but soon there *was* no off-season.

A number of high schools and colleges around the country began scheduling programs at the Teton Science School. Flo Krall, environmental education expert at the University of Utah, under whom I had worked for a year as an adjunct instructor, began taking her classes to the Teton Science School for special programs. One included author Terry Tempest Williams, one of the students I took down the river in 1973.

Before long the school developed a program of professional residency in environmental education and natural science. Its brochure advertises "Learning Adventures in Science for Young People and Adults" in the spectacular setting of the Tetons on a secluded campus, once a dude ranch, which retains much of its western character. Ted and Joan have retired and now live on the west side of the Tetons near Victor, Idaho, but they retain a close association with the Teton Science School. I teach an adult course, "The Nature of Rivers," there every summer.

Canoeist Paul Huser takes a break below the mouth of the Gros Ventre River against the backdrop of the Teton Range. The exposed river cobble suggests a late-summer low-water level good for fishing. Photo by Verne Huser.

The Moose-to-Wilson stretch of river, roughly fourteen miles of Classes I and II river, remains popular with fishermen and some scenic floaters, though the more spectacular scenery lies upstream in the park. I like to canoe this stretch of river, but except in spring and fall I see less wildlife there, fewer large animals and birds. Once the dikes close in, the natural quality of the river deteriorates, but some wildlife continues: flocks of ducks and geese, seasonal herds of elk, plenty of big fat mule deer, an occasional moose. Autumn color offers a special treat from late September through mid-October, depending on temperatures and weather patterns. Fishing improves with lower water levels—remember, this is a reservoir-release river controlled by irrigation demands in Idaho, and the farmers are already harvesting the potato crop.

The Gros Ventre (pronounced grow-*vont*) River enters just north of West Gros Ventre Butte on the left about ten miles from Moose—only four miles to go to the Wilson Bridge river access and a possible takeout. Dikes bind the river tighter and tighter as civilization encroaches ever more on the riverine environment.

From the Wilson Bridge access, it is thirteen miles to the next official river access point at South Park Landing. Below the Wilson

Gravel was once mined directly from the Snake River.
Photo by Verne Huser.

Bridge the Snake divides even more, hugs the west side of the valley, splitting and meandering through a broader floodplain. Fish Creek, which drains much of the lower Teton Range eastward and flows through the town of Wilson, enters the Snake from the right (west) about three miles below the bridge. Mosquito Creek (where an old sawmill operated for decades) and another creek named Cottonwood enter only a few hundred yards apart, about two miles below the mouth of Fish Creek. Below Cottonwood Creek the river takes a decided turn to the southeast, the result of a major cross-fault that reverses the tilt of the valley floor, and Taylor Creek enters another mile downstream. I have hunted elk and deer—never killed any but had nice outings—in the high country drained by these tributaries.

All of these streams enter from the west, flowing off the hills above the river. The Snake River Range begins south of Teton Pass, a low point on the divide west of Jackson Hole that marks the southern limit of the Teton Range. East of the river is Flat Creek, which heads above the National Elk Refuge, flows through the town of Jackson, and parallels the Snake, picking up water from minor tributaries to the east. Spring Creek, which drains the ranchland between East and West Gros Ventre Buttes and flows the length of South Park, enters the Snake from the east two miles below Taylor Creek on the opposite side. The Snake flows through so many different channels in South Park that a tributary entering the river

Von Gontard's Landing where the highway crosses the Snake at the lower end of South Park. Photo by Verne Huser.

from one side or the other may not be seen directly by a party on the main river, only felt in increased flow when the channel enters below the next island.

Dikes often divide the Snake from its natural offspring, the small ponds and acres of wetlands that border the river in South Park. So porous is the cobble of the riverbed that water bleeds into adjacent areas despite the dikes. Five full miles below the confluence of Spring Creek with the Snake, Flat Creek finally enters the main river. A cross-fault has tilted the lower end of the valley in South Park to the east, turning the Snake eastward and allowing Flat Creek, which has paralleled the Snake for a dozen miles, to join the Snake.

Gravel was once mined directly out of the river in this whole stretch, increasing its turbidity, but environmental laws have finally put an end to that practice. Lew Clark, who ran one of the largest sand and gravel operations in Teton County, once told me that even though he had first fought these environmental restrictions, he found they made sense and improved his business, making it more profitable and certainly less intrusive upon the natural environment, a benefit he appreciated more and more as he saw the positive results. My classes in the "River Resource" at the Teton Science School in the early 1980s always visited Lew's sand and gravel operation.

Through South Park—an area rapidly filling with homes and people—evening beavers abound. Ducks and geese raise young, then flock for migration, and great blue heron fly ahead of any raft, canoe, kayak, or dory on the river. About ten miles below the Wilson Bridge, the Snake gradually swings to the left (east), eventually—in three or four miles—nudging the valley's eastern wall to turn south past Hog Island on the right bank.

Von Gontard's Landing, the bridge crossing U.S. 26/89/187/189, also known as South Park Landing, is less than a dozen miles south of the town of Jackson. The Wyoming Game and Fish Department maintains a winter elk-feeding area between Flat Creek and the Snake on what amounts to the left bank of the Snake a mile above this access point. In the fall of 1995 a grizzly bear sow and three cubs were seen in South Park. The sow chased a man on horseback. When local wildlife authorities attempted to tranquilize the bears, one of the cubs fell into the water and drowned before it could be captured; the other three bears were moved into the wilderness.

Despite its braiding and meandering throughout South Park, the Snake once more flows in a single channel at the access beneath the bridge and maintains this common flow as it enters the canyon. This segment of Snake River has been impacted by human activity and development more than any other stretch of river in Jackson Hole, but it too offers rewards to anyone willing to ply its braided channels.

Section 6 (30 miles)

The Canyon—
South Park to Palisades Reservoir

Many authorities mark the beginning of Grand Canyon of the Snake River at the mouth of Hoback River, but for me it begins just below the confluence of Flat Creek with the Snake. The most popular boating stretch of the Snake outside Grand Teton National Park, the lower part of this segment sees well over one hundred thousand floaters a season, largely paddle rafters and kayakers. It is heavily fished in the fall, when spectacular autumn colors decorate the canyon's aspens, cottonwoods, and mountain maples.

At Von Gontard's Landing beneath the highway bridge (U.S. 26/89/187/189) immediately below the confluence of Flat Creek with the Snake, many fishing and scenic float trips leave the river after floating through South Park. Below this landing adjacent terrain steepens, first on the left bank, then on the right, and finally on both sides as the Snake approaches its confluence with Hoback River, a major tributary that has created its own minor canyon. The surrounding country consists of deep sediments and glacial cobble that form high, flat terraces. These benches terminate in the highlands that form the eastern-most flank of the Gros Ventre Range. Aspen groves dominate the unstable, undulating terrain characterized by carpet slumps, landslides that are similar to slab avalanches in snow.

The Old Highway, subject to frequent but minor landslides and winter avalanches, follows the left bank. When the main road hung on the east edge of the river, Hog Island, an alluvial fan on the right bank where several families traditionally farmed or ranched, was accessible only across a suspension bridge that scared the wits out of most nonresidents, one reason the area was considered an island—it was relatively inaccessible.

This bridge was known as the Swinging Bridge for its tendency to sway with the wind or with any vehicle on its deck. Replaced by

The Old Swinging Bridge across the Snake River was for years the main access to Hog Island. The modern highway lies on the Hog Island side of the Snake. Courtesy of the Jackson Hole Historical Society.

a new bridge (actually a section of an earlier bridge across the Snake between Jackson and Wilson) several decades ago, the old Swinging Bridge created a host of stories related to its apparent instability, but to my knowledge it never precipitated anyone into the river.

The new bridge now provides access to residences on the left bank since the new highway lies on the Hog Island side of the river. Hog Island has experienced increased development during recent years. In a sense, today's residents on the left bank now live in isolation on their own little island. A pair of osprey has nested for years on the superstructure of the new bridge, but authorities moved the nest to a safer location the spring of 1998, an apparently successful transplant.

Between the South Park Landing and Hoback River, Porcupine Creek and Horse Creek enter from the left. A quartet of small streams that head on Munger Mountain (8,383 feet) and flow through Hog Island—Bohnetts Creek, Dells Creek, Georges Creek, and Coles Creek (all reportedly named for local residents)—enter from the right. The canyon grows gradually deeper as it approaches the Hoback, which often flows muddier than the Snake because its headwaters lie in an area of unstable landforms. Lewis Landing, a river access, lies on the left bank just above the mouth of Hoback River, which has become increasingly popular with whitewater paddlers, especially kayakers, in recent years.

In *Astoria,* his account of the John Jacob Astor venture of 1811–1812, Washington Irving wrote, "Here Hoback's River was joined by a river [the Snake] of great magnitude and swifter current and their united waters swept through the valley in one impetuous stream, which from its rapidity and turbulence, had received the name of Mad River." Members of the party, seeing the river in September, tried to continue their journey to the mouth of the Columbia by water, but they found the Snake uncooperative.

Three miles downstream the Astorians camped for several days, trying to decide whether to continue by water or go overland. They hunted, cut cottonwood trees to build dugout canoes, and explored the area. After a dugout canoe crafted to negotiate the river capsized and wrecked on October 20, 1811, they chose the overland route, led over Teton Pass by friendly Shoshone Indians.

At this confluence a small community known as Hoback Junction continues to grow, with handsome homes rising on any privately owned land in the vicinity; most of the surrounding land lies in the Bridger-Teton National Forest. The main highway through Hoback Canyon (U.S. 189/191), a scenic road through a steep landscape, offers frequent opportunities to see bighorn sheep near Stinking Springs as well as congregated mule deer during winter months.

Every year more river runners boat the Hoback, which can be a dangerous run at high water with new obstacles often appearing overnight. Several fatalities have occurred in recent decades, for the river offers some challenging whitewater.

A major tributary, Granite Creek, attracted an Earth First! gathering in the early 1980s. Ed Abbey, Earth First! founder, famed author, and one of the best-known advocates of monkey wrenching—attended to protest oil drilling in the Granite Creek drainage, part of the exploration boom in the Overthrust Belt that threatened to turn Teton County into a zone of petrochemical exploitation. Granite Creek's massive drainage heads in the Gros Ventre Range, initially flows northeast, then curves in a huge arch to enter the Hoback in a southwesterly direction, forming a near-perfect twenty-mile crescent.

From Hoback Junction the Snake flows southwest, zigging and zagging a bit below the mouth of Fall Creek, which drains major elk habitat to the west and enters the Snake from the right less than a half mile below and within sight of the Hoback. The Hoback River sometimes runs red with muddy tributary sediments into a green Snake River; Fall Creek adds a brownish silt, and for a short distance the Snake flows in tricolored confusion.

In the early 1980s, Edward Abbey attended an Earth First! gathering on Granite Creek to protest oil and gas exploration—and the appearance of rigs such as the one pictured on the right—in the Overthrust Belt. Granite Creek flows into the Hoback River, a major Snake River tributary. Photos by Verne Huser.

Between steeply rising canyon walls the Snake flows, swirls, and eddies in an open S-curve for three miles to Astoria Hot Springs on the left bank. A modern swimming pool, picnic area, and camp-

ground occupied the site until 2000, an area known locally as Johnny Counts Flats for an early settler and miner.

The Snake bends sharply to the southeast immediately below Astoria Hot Springs as the canyon widens and the river begins to split into several channels. The stretch from Astoria Hot Springs to the Elbow, not challenging enough for most kayakers and not subject to the commercial masses, has become increasingly popular with private floaters. Prichard Landing on the right bank a mile below Astoria Hot Springs provides access. The Snake River gets downright crowded at times with more than one hundred thousand floaters in the canyon every summer.

A word here about the lay of the land: from the bridge crossing the Snake at Moose, the Snake River flows essentially south in a kind of open-fishhook pattern, the point open and facing east—until it reaches South Park Landing. At this point the river approaches the Snake River Range, which it bisects in a zigzag pattern, a huge, irregular backward S—until it reaches the obvious elbow at the mouth of Bailey Creek where the river takes a decided turn to the west.

At this point a spur of the Wyoming Range intrudes from the south and, rising to the east in a long, high ridge (Greyback Ridge), essentially forces the Snake River westward. Below the end of the canyon, both Gray's River (from the east) and the Salt River (from the south) enter Palisades Reservoir, formed by the damming of the Snake several miles downstream in Idaho. Palisades Dam backs water into the lower Snake River Canyon, inundating several miles of river, a few minor rapids, and the Narrows, where the Snake flows through a thirty-foot slot.

A mile below Prichard Landing the Snake bumps into the right bank, which carries the main highway through the canyon, (U.S. 26/89) just below the mouth of Dog Creek where a major landslide blocked the road for several weeks in the spring of 1997, forcing the river left and altering its course for several miles. The spring of 1998 the slide again seeped muddy water.

For the next five miles the river hugs the right bank, a steep, forested hillside that still carries the road through the canyon. A number of bald eagles that nest in the canyon can often be seen there, soaring over the river, perched in a riverside fir, spruce, or cottonwood or diving for fish. The left bank, low and flat for the first three and a half miles, has been mined for gold, although not very successfully. However, it grows a good crop of cottonwoods through which occasional high-water channels meander, forming temporary islands. Livestock graze these flats.

Bailey Creek enters the Snake from the left as the river makes a sharp right-hand turn and heads west. An old, rusty World War II amphibious landing craft with a cargo and troop-carrying bay and gigantic tank treads lies back in the willows, half-buried in river silt. Tradition holds that it was used in a gold-mining operation—some say a scam—shortly after the war.

An old prospector built his tiny log cabin on the left bank of the river and lived there from 1887 to 1911, a kind, generous man running away from his past that included killing a fellow miner in a saloon brawl in Virginia City, Montana. According to Fritiof Fryxell's account in *American Forests* (October 1935), Uncle Jack Davis eked out a modest living by panning for gold in the Snake River gravel and the sands of Bailey Creek.

So repentant had Jack become over the killing in Montana, he refused to kill anything, even for food, and became a vegetarian. His old burro, Calamity Jane, lived to be forty years old, and bluebirds nested in his cabin. Several of his pets—Lucy, the doe; Dan, his horse; and Pitchfork Tillman, one of his cats—outlived Uncle Jack, who died a poor man on March 25, 1911.

The Elbow marks the beginning of the deepest, steepest, most spectacular part of the canyon where the real whitewater exists. Seven of twenty-six recreation sites listed in and marked on the official Forest Service Bridger-Teton National Forest Map are located in the thirteen-mile stretch between the Elbow and Palisades Reservoir.

The summers of 1972 and 1973 Barker-Ewing began its whitewater float trips at the Forest Service's Elbow Campground, but because commercial river use began to crowd out the general public, the Forest Service developed an official river access two miles downstream at West Table Creek, a better launch site with more room for parking and orientation, but we missed our first minor rapid. However, a perfect geologic feature, a small but prominent anticline, lies across the river from this access, giving guides a good excuse to talk about the geology of the canyon that the river carved through ancient limestone beds.

Less than a mile below the West Table Creek launch site rapids begin in a ledge system called Fence Rapid immediately below Station Creek Campground on the right bank. (The highway is on the riverbank, and so are all road-related features.) At low water one summer a boat became stranded on an exposed part of this ledge system; its passengers milled around on the ledge for a couple hours, then finally decided to swim to shore. One young woman never made it: sucked out of her life jacket, she drowned.

The S-turns follow in quick succession, a series of small ledge-formed rapids in a rockbound canyon. This section requires careful maneuvering; the small drops can be misleading. On one of my trips with an adventuresome group, I talked about the keeper quality of pour-overs—the tendency of the water to flow upstream to fill the holes created by a rapid. They wanted to experience the

The S-turns lie just above the major whitewater rapids in the Snake River Canyon immediately below Fence Rapid. Photo by Verne Huser.

phenomenon. I took the next little pour-over, a drop of less than two feet, sideways. We stopped dead, caught in the backflow. Never in any danger of flipping, we nonetheless felt the awesome power of the reverse current. One of the passengers timed us: we stayed in the keeper for fifty-seven seconds until I rowed us out.

A large keeper on the right side of the river in the S-turns is known as Taco Hole for a raft that folded in half like a taco with its passengers trapped in the middle like so much meat, cheese, lettuce, and tomatoes. It is a favorite play spot for kayakers.

A couple of aspects of this stretch bear mentioning: the Dinosaur Back, a sharp ridge of rock a mile below Station Creek Campground that appears right of center as water levels drop (you have to work hard to miss it at certain flows), and the Big Eddy (also known as Otter Eddy for a family of river otters that appears several times a summer), an area with powerful eddies on both sides of the main current in the wide pool where Iron Rim Creek enters the Snake. In-experienced paddlers and rowers may spend several minutes trying to find the downstream current.

The Iron Rim is a two-mile long cliff wall, part of a huge over-thrust of bedrock, a dramatic formation from the river, even more obvious from the highway above. Three-Oar-Deal, a massive, pow-erful, left-of-center hydraulic that most experienced river runners avoid, is formed by the river's course through that formation. Squir-

Rafts on approach to the Three-Oar-Deal Rapid below Iron Rim Creek.
Photo by Verne Huser.

relly hydraulics characterize the big Wolf Creek pool. A family of
beavers once had a bank den in this huge pool just above the mouth
of the creek.

Below Wolf Creek are the Gauging Straights, a mile-long straight
stretch marked by a gauging station cable across the river. Numerous large avalanche paths mark the steep left bank of this stretch.
During early season trips floaters find large pyramids of snow at
river level, remnants of winter avalanches.

This riffled stretch prepares passengers for bigger and badder
rapids around the next corner at Blind Canyon. Water ouzel sometimes nest on the big riverside rock on the right at the lower end of
the Straights. A small curler on the right—it is easy to miss—offers
a good cold splash in anticipation of Big Kahuna, followed by
Lunch Counter around the bend.

Kahuna and Lunch Counter alternate as best rapids depending
on water levels. Kahuna is biggest at water levels of 4,500 to 6,500
cubic feet per second (cfs); above that Kahuna begins to wash out.
At certain low-water levels Kahuna can be a killer rapid because its
big curl-back wave can stop a boat dead, throwing its passengers
violently forward and into the water, which is shallow and full
of rocks; it is best to avoid the big hole in Kahuna at such low-flow
levels.

Lunch Counter is the most feared rapid in the Canyon. Because it

A paddle raft runs the rapid known as Big Kahuna in the Snake River Canyon. Photo by Verne Huser.

is created by a combination of underwater ledges and current constriction through a narrow slot, it reacts differently at varying flow levels. From 9,000 to 10,000 cfs, Lunch Counter has a broad tongue that leads to a set of thrilling cross-folding tail waves. At 12,000 to 16,000 cfs, the lead waves disappear, but the tail waves increase in intensity. From 16,000 to 19,000 cfs, it starts flipping boats, especially when the wind is up. Even an experienced professional guide who knows the river well and has a perfect line can flip there, especially on windy days when the bottom of the boat rising above the big wave in Lunch Counter catches the wind from downstream. The tail waves pulsate in a chaotic pattern impossible to predict.

Above 20,000 cfs Lunch Counter tends to wash out, the river inundating the constricting ledges, creating a seething, boiling depression in the wide current. At high-water levels Barker-Ewing at one time maintained a powerboat in the huge eddy below Lunch Counter as a safety measure to pick up swimmers who had been knocked out of boats or from boats that had flipped.

Lunch Counter's waves have become a popular surfing area. Surfers on surfboards ride the waves between float trips, and kayakers love to play in the conflicting currents. At times it is more difficult to avoid boats coming downstream than it is to catch the waves. Remember that in contrast to ocean waves, river waves remain stationary. With the consistency of Lunch Counter's big waves at cer-

The guide, standing at the oars, rows a self-bailing boat through Lunch Counter Rapid in the Snake River Canyon. Photo by Verne Huser.

tain water levels, this rapid offers an easy, accessible surfing site miles from any ocean.

Around the next bend to the left lies Rope Rapid, a series of waves that offers a roller-coaster ride at most water levels, but at high water it can become a serious problem as the current takes over. Then comes Champagne at another series of limestone ledges: at low water it is merely frothy, bubbly, but at higher water the limestone ledge becomes an island. I have seen a free-floating forty-foot log a half meter in diameter caught in the conflicting currents for three days.

Another S-bend, first to the left, then to the right, and you are into Cottonwood Rapid, the last and longest—and some think, the most dangerous—rapid in the canyon. On the left bank at the head of Cottonwood stands a well-worn dead tree atop a limestone cliff, a favorite jumping spot for daredevils. People take dangerous risks here, leaping into the river from the tree, despite shallow ledges and curious currents. Several years ago a man jumped in and did not resurface. He was not wearing a personal flotation device.

The river does crazy things in this final rapid. As water levels fluctuate, the safe runs change with different flows, and any course through the rocky rapid requires maneuvering. After negotiating Cottonwood the only worry is making the Forest Service takeout on the right bank at Sheep Gulch. As most river runners do not appreciate rowing or paddling on flat water, it pays to catch this well-developed river access—the facilities are obvious, and crowds of people normally mark it well.

At Sheep Gulch, perhaps 140 river miles from the farthest headwater spring of the Snake, you are 104 river miles from the South Entrance of Yellowstone National Park, 78 river miles from Jackson Lake Dam, about 900 river miles from the confluence with the Columbia, and still well over 1,200 miles from the Pacific.

Sheep Gulch marks a steep, stony, V-shaped drainage fed by melting snows from the east face of Ferry Peak, which dominates the skyline to the northwest of the canyon. Its sedimentary cliff walls and golden pyramid summit provide habitat for a small herd of transplanted mountain goats.

If you miss the takeout, you must go all the way to the reservoir, and that means running the Narrows. At high river flows and low lake level it can be a killer. The Narrows is the tightest constriction on the whole Upper Snake; the entire flow of the Snake pours through a narrow gap, accompanied by great turbulence and violent, unpredictable hydraulics. There is a boat ramp at Palisades Marina on the left bank just below the mouth of Gray's River but upstream from the bridge. However, it is only usable when reservoir levels are above 5,600-feet elevation (the reservoir is full at 5,620 feet).

Palisades Reservoir turns the Snake into a lake, yet another drowned river. As the river dies in the reservoir, the mountains recede and the canyon ends in a small valley where Alpine Junction marks the confluence of both Gray's River and Salt River with the Snake.

The violent geologic forces that produced the steep, folded mountains that border the Snake are permanently recorded in the twisted and buckled ribbons of gray sedimentary rocks on the left side of the river, eroded into towers, arches, and caves—a proper setting, perhaps, for the Snake's dying throes.

A Word to Readers

Naturally, historically, environmentally, geologically the Upper Snake River in Wyoming links Grand Teton and Yellowstone National Parks more meaningfully than the modern roads most park visitors now use to access the parks. Certainly, one of the best ways to get to know the parks intimately is on the river, rafting or canoeing the Snake in Grand Teton National Park or the John D. Rockefeller Jr. Memorial Parkway, or canoeing the tributary Lewis River in Yellowstone.

As visitation to the parks and their connecting parkway rises, river use tends to increase even more rapidly, especially among private paddlers, the result of more people discovering the area from the river and passing on their new insights and enjoyment by word of mouth. Today a quarter-million people float the Snake River in northwest Wyoming every summer.

The busloads of tourists and drive-through visitors to Jackson Hole normally float the Snake River with commercial outfitters, but more and more died-in-the-wool outdoorsmen bring their canoes, kayaks, and rafts along on their vacations to explore the rivers on their own—and on its own terms. More fishermen appear every year with their rafts and dories to ply the waters of the Upper Snake.

What better way to examine the geologic features, see the evolving wildflower display, find fish or wildlife in a natural setting, explore the history, and study the ecology than to experience the river firsthand, either on your own or with a knowledgeable guide? What better way to explore the valley beneath the Teton peaks than by water, which has played so vital a role in its formation?

During recent decades while use of the Snake River has increased, both in Grand Teton National Park and in the Snake River Canyon, the administering agencies, the National Park Service and the U.S. Forest Service, have attempted to control use and reduce its impact on the river and its fauna and flora.

Though scenic commercial float trips are restricted from landing along the river except at specifically designated sites (river access areas), fishing trips are allowed to stop and fish. Many of them essentially day-camp, stopping along the river to occupy the shore while they fish, lunch, and relax. Such activities trample riverbank vegetation, disturb wildlife, alter birds' nesting and nurturing activities, and reduce the wild character of the river corridor. They spoil the area for scenic floaters. Fishermen, on the other hand, dislike the constant stream of scenic floaters who drift by, spoiling their fishing, scaring the fish away from their favorite holes, and ruining their solitude.

Can the two river users coexist? Both segments have the right to use the river. How can they best be accommodated? Do we need more rules? Do we need stricter enforcement of existing rules? As both groups increase, something positive needs to be done to prevent the situation from getting out of hand, to prevent the river users from destroying the quality of the experience for all interested parties and of the nature of the river itself.

My personal solution is antipodal paddling, running the river when and where others seldom venture. I like to be on the river at dawn or dusk when I have the river to myself or in the off-season, in the fall when most tourists have gone home or in the spring before they arrive. I have even canoed the Snake in the winter, participating in the Audubon Christmas Bird Count; I saw no one else on the river that day. I have also run a few moonlight trips; I do not suggest you try that unless you know the river as well as I did then. I would not try it myself now.

Another problem is that some float trip operations and some guides row their passengers down the river rather than floating with the current, a practice that increases both guide and outfitter income (they can haul more people down the river) as well as visitor contact with other groups. Such activity detracts from the wilderness experience of everyone who floats the Snake.

If every boat on the river floated with the speed of the current and launched out of sight of the next boat (as park regulations suggest), few passengers would see another boat, except for a few fishermen and the large, heavy pontoons, which catch more current and thus float faster. These larger, heavier boats are a generally accepted part of the tradition of river running on the Snake: they were the boats used in the first commercial scenic float trips. Fishermen, too, are part of traditional river use.

Although overuse of the river resource threatens to degrade the quality of the river experience, other threats exist as well: clear-cut logging at the headwaters of tributary streams; overdevelopment on the riverbank and in the floodplain; building dikes along the river, thereby not only restricting its natural meandering patterns but also limiting its ability to flood naturally, necessarily; overgrazing in the watershed; mining activities; and inappropriate agricultural practices. In resonse to pressure, the U.S. Army Corps of Engineers (ACE) is making environmental restoration studies. Given that wealthy landowners who have built trophy homes along the river within the floodplain also have abundant political clout, it is unlikely the dikes will soon disappear. At this time, the ACE in considering only creating some backwaters.

Most of the Upper Snake River lies within jurisdiction of the Grand Teton National Park and the Bridger-Teton National Forest. If you are concerned about the quality of your experience on the Snake and in the preservation of its natural beauty, you might want to write to the following agencies and copy your letter to your own congressional representatives:

Superintendent   Supervisor
Grand Teton National Park   Bridger-Teton National Forest
P.O. Drawer 170   P.O. Box 1888
Moose, WY 83012   Jackson, WY 83001

Sources and Suggested Reading

Bonney, Lorraine G. 1992. *The Grand Controversy.* New York: AAC Press.
———. 1995. *Bonney's Guide to Jackson's Hole and Grand Teton National Park.* Moose, Wyo.: Homestead Publishing.
Carrighar, Sally. 1947. *One Day on Teton Marsh.* New York: Alfred A. Knopf.
Chittenden, Hiram M. 1986. *The American Fur Trade of the Far West.* Lincoln: University of Nebraska Press.
Clark, Tim W. 1999. *Ecology of Jackson Hole, Wyoming.* Moose, Wyo.: Grand Teton Natural History Association.
Craighead, Charlie. 1994. *The Eagle and the River.* New York: Simon and Schuster.
———. 1997. *"Who Ate the Backyard?": Living with Wildlife on Private Land.* Moose, Wyo.: Grand Teton Natural History Association.
Craighead, Frank C., Jr. 1963. *For Everything There Is a Season.* Helena: Falcon.
———. 1982. *Track of the Grizzly.* San Francisco: Sierra Club.
Craighead, John J., Frank C. Craighead Jr., and Ray J. Davis. 1963. *A Field Guide to Rocky Mountain Wildflowers.* Boston: Houghton Mifflin.
Fabian, Josephine C. 1955. *Jackson Hole: How to Discover and Enjoy It.* Self-published.
Fryxell, Fritiof. 1959. *The Tetons: Interpretation of a Mountain Landscape.* Berkeley: University of California Press.
Koch, Edward D., and Charles R. Peterson. 1995. *Amphibians and Reptiles of Yellowstone and Grand Teton National Parks.* Salt Lake City: University of Utah Press.
Laubin, Reginald, and Gladys Laubin. 1957. *The Indian Tipi.* Norman: University of Oklahoma Press.
———. 1977. *Indian Dances of North America.* Norman: University of Oklahoma Press.
———. 1980. *American Indian Archery.* Norman: University of Oklahoma Press.
Love, J. D., and John C. Reed Jr. 1989. *Creation of the Teton Landscape.* Moose, Wyo.: Grand Teton Natural History Association.
McDougall, W. B., and Herman A. Baggley. 1956. *The Plants of Yellowstone National Park.* Yellowstone Park, Wyo.: Yellowstone Library and Museum Association.
McPhee, John. 1986. *Rising from the Plains.* New York: Farrar, Straus, and Giroux, the Noonday Press.

Morgan, Dale. 1964. *Jedediah Smith and the Opening of the West*. Lincoln: University of Nebraska Press.

Murie, Adolph. 1940. *Ecology of the Coyote in the Yellowstone*. Fauna Series, no. 4. Washington, D.C.: National Park Service.

Murie, Margaret, and Olaus Murie. 1967. *Wapiti Wilderness*. New York: Alfred A. Knopf.

Murie, Olaus. 1951. *The Elk of North America*. Harrisburg: Wildlife Management Institute.

———. 1954. *A Field Guide to Animal Tracks*. Boston: Houghton Mifflin.

———. 1963. *Jackson Hole with a Naturalist*. Jackson Hole: Frontier Press.

Nash, Roderick. 1967. *Wilderness and the American Mind*. New Haven: Yale University Press.

———. 1989. *The Rights of Nature*. Madison: University of Wisconsin Press.

National Park Service. 1984. *Grand Teton: A Guide to Grand Teton National Park, Wyoming*. Washington, D.C.: National Park Service.

Palmer, Tim. 1991. *The Snake River: Window to the West*. Washington, D.C.: Island Press.

———. 1997. *The Columbia River: Sustaining a Modern Resource*. Seattle: The Mountaineers.

Raynes, Bert. 1984. *Birds of Grand Teton National Park and the Surrounding Area*. Moose, Wyo.: Grand Teton Natural History Association.

Righter, Robert W. 1982. *Crucible for Conservation: The Struggle for Grand Teton National Park*. Boulder: Colorado Associated University Press.

———. 1990. *A Teton County Anthology*. Roberts Rinehart.

Russell, Osborne. 1965. *Journal of a Trapper, 1834–1843*. Lincoln: University of Nebraska Press.

Saylor, David J. 1971. *Jackson Hole, Wyoming: In the Shadow of the Tetons*. Norman: University of Oklahoma Press.

Shaw, Richard J. 1981. *Plants of Yellowstone and Grand Teton National Parks*. Salt Lake City: Wheelwright Press.

Talbot, Vivian Linford. 1996. *David E. Jackson: Field Captain of the Rocky Mountain Fur Trade*. Jackson: Jackson Hole Historical Society and Museum.

Thompson, Edith M., and William Leigh Thompson. 1982. *Beaver Dick: The Honor and the Heartbreak*. Laramie, Wyo.: Jehm Mountain Press.

Index

Wolves of Mount McKinley, The
  (Murie, 1944), 75
woodpeckers, 91, 93
Wyeth, Nathaniel J., 10
Wyoming Game and Fish Depart-
  ment, 83, 180
Wyoming Range, 186

yellow-headed blackbirds, 85, *86*
yellow monkey flower, 71, 72
Yellowstone National Park:
  conservation movement and expansion of, 23; establishment of,
  12; and float trips on Snake River,
  127–32; and Nez Perce Indians, 6;
  and Snake River system, ix
yellow warblers, 85